# In the Chair

| DATE DUE | | | |
|---|---|---|---|
|  |  |  |  |
|  |  |  |  |
|  |  |  |  |
|  |  |  |  |
|  |  |  |  |
|  |  |  |  |
|  |  |  |  |
|  |  |  |  |
|  |  |  |  |
|  |  |  |  |
|  |  |  |  |
|  |  |  |  |

Andrew Green was born in 1952 and educated at schools in Yorkshire and at the University of Cambridge. He trained as a professional librarian and worked in various universities in Wales and England, culminating in the post of Director of Library and Information Services in the University of Wales Swansea. From 1998 to 2013 he was Librarian or Chief Executive of the National Library of Wales, one of the five legal deposit libraries of the UK and a major archive repository. He has acted as Chair of a large number of voluntary, public sector and official bodies, and currently chairs the Board of Coleg Cenedlaethol Cymru, the national body responsible for organising higher education through the medium of the Welsh language. Andrew has published and lectured widely on digital, information and cultural subjects.

www.gwallter.com

@gwallter

# In the Chair

*How to Guide Groups
and Manage Meetings*

Andrew Green

Parthian
The Old Surgery
Napier Street
Cardigan
SA43 1ED

www.parthianbooks.com

First published in 2014
© Andrew Green 2014
All Rights Reserved

ISBN 978-1909844780

Cover design by Marc Jennings at www.theundercard.co.uk
Typeset by Elaine Sharples
Printed and bound by Gwasg Gomer, Llandysul
Illustrations © Juta Tirona at www.jutatirona.com

Published with the financial support of the Welsh Books
Council

British Library Cataloguing in Publication Data
A cataloguing record for this book is available from the
British Library.

# Contents

Foreword                                                            xi

Chapter 1 **Does the chair fit?**                                    **1**
  1.1   Groups and meetings: burden or benefit?         3
  1.2   Why have groups? Why hold meetings?             4
  1.3   What's a chair for?                             7
  1.4   What skills does a chair need?                  8
  1.5   What knowledge does a chair need?              17
  1.6   What are the chair's functions?                18
  1.7   How do I learn to be a good chair?             19

Chapter 2 **Knowing your role**                                     **21**
  2.1   How do you get to be chair?                    23
  2.2   The context                                    24
  2.3   The group's aims                               26
  2.4   The group's members                            28
  2.5   How the group will operate                     34
  2.6   How the group will behave                      35

Chapter 3 **Planning the meeting**                                  **39**
  3.1   Do you need a meeting?                          41
  3.2   Place and time                                 42
  3.3   Duration                                       42
  3.4   The agenda                                     44
  3.5   Communicating with the members                 49
  3.6   Preparing the environment                      51
  3.7   Preparing yourself                             53

## Chapter 4 **Conducting the meeting, 1: mechanics**　　　**57**

4.1　Before the meeting starts　　59
4.2　Introducing the meeting　　60
4.3　Timing and the agenda　　63
4.4　Standard agenda items, 1: minutes and matters arising　　64
4.5　Standard agenda items, 2: papers and presentations　　66
4.6　Standard agenda items, 3: reports　　67
4.7　Standard agenda items, 4: any other business　　68

## Chapter 5 **Conducting the meeting, 2: dynamics**　　　**71**

5.1　Orchestrating discussion　　73
5.2　Influencing the direction of discussion　　76
5.3　Influencing the flow of discussion　　80
5.4　Influencing the understanding of a discussion　　84
5.5　Reaching decisions　　86
5.6　Concluding the meeting　　91
5.7　Following up the meeting　　92

## Chapter 6 **Chairs, boards and chief executives**　　　**95**

6.1　Chairing the board of a public body　　97
6.2　Chairing the board of a company　　101
6.3　Working with a chief executive　　105
6.4　The functions of the board　　109
6.5　Meetings of the board　　112
6.6　Representing the board and the organisation　　115
6.7　Evaluating the board's performance　　116

## Chapter 7 **Special kinds of groups and meetings**　　　**119**

7.1　Formal meetings　　121
7.2　Annual meetings　　124
7.3　Conferences　　128
7.4　Public meetings　　132
7.5　Appointment panels　　137

7.6   Quasi-judicial meetings: disciplinary and
      grievance hearings                              141
7.7   Facilitating                                    144
7.8   Bilingual and multilingual meetings             147
7.9   Remote meetings: teleconferences and
      videoconferences                                149

**Chapter 8 Looking back and looking forward**       **153**

A chairing checklist: 10 'dos' and 'don'ts'          157

Further reading                                       161

Index                                                 168

# Foreword

There are hundreds, if not thousands, of books about leadership. Most of them are about how to act as a leader who has executive power – typically, the chief executive of a company or a public body, or the holder of political or military office. Only a few focus on a different kind of leader, namely one who doesn't have the dominant authority or status of a director or chief executive but who uses influence primarily through coordinating, orchestrating and persuading other people. The term most commonly used for this position is 'chair'.

The important thing about chairs is that the power they exercise is not concentrated and unconstrained. It's qualified, and shared with others – the members of the group they lead. Even when vested with real powers a chair may choose not to wield them, but to rely on other means of influence.

In the same way as physical chairs vary, from impressive padded armchairs to humble three-legged wooden stools, so organisational chairs differ widely according to the sort of group of which they're in charge. The group may be a multi-million pound company, a public board, a parliamentary select committee or a small community association. The group's nature, powers and composition are of central importance to the chair. So too is the way the group operates, which is usually through coming together to discuss and decide the matters it's responsible for – that is, through holding meetings. This is why the chair is most often thought of in the context of managing meetings. A common definition of a chair is 'the person who presides over a meeting'.

Hearts often sink when the word 'meeting' is mentioned. The reasons are obvious enough. Meetings are too often associated with negatives like boredom, irrelevance, conflict or pointlessness. They're a substitute for 'real' work. The author Michael Foley summarises a common worker's view of them like this:

Employees hate meetings because they reveal that self-promotion, sycophancy, dissimulation and constantly talking nonsense in a loud confident voice are more impressive than merely being good at the job – and it is depressing to lack these skills but even more depressing to discover one's self using them.[1]

But it doesn't have to be like that. Meetings can be interesting or even engrossing, and rewarding in spirit and in outcome. There is, though, one thing that makes a critical difference between a positive and a negative experience: the way a meeting is chaired. A badly managed meeting is almost certain to depress all the participants and reduce their contributions. A well-run meeting will allow them to leave the room feeling fulfilled, having achieved some common goals. They may even approach the next meeting with hope rather than foreboding.

So this book is about the skills of chairing: managing groups, and especially managing the meetings where they come together. It looks at both from the point of view of the person in charge. It's based on two firm beliefs:

• that good chairing makes for effective groups and efficient, even enjoyable, meetings
• that it's possible to learn the skills needed to be an excellent chair

There have been several good guides to successful chairing (mainly chairing meetings) over the years. But time doesn't stand still, and the practice of chairing has changed. For one thing,

---

[1] Michael Foley, *Embracing the Ordinary: Lessons from the Champions of Everyday Life*, London: Simon & Schuster, 2012, p.244.

we've all become less respectful of authority and deferential to hierarchy, so the chair will not command automatic reverence. People expect to be able to have their say and to have their views respected. Formal meetings, with their points of order and amendments to motions, are rarer, and informal meetings more common. Time seems more precious, and the iron discipline of 'cost-effectiveness' binds almost everyone, so that languorous debate is something few can afford. And meeting technologies have evolved: people don't have to be in the same room, or even in the same country, to hold a meeting.

This book, then, is for the contemporary chair. It's aimed at those new to the position, but it should also interest those who already have some experience. Chief executives may find it helpful: they often act as chairs themselves, and may be responsible to the chair of a board of directors. And any member of a meeting should gain something from reading it. It's designed to be read through with comparative ease, but also to be mined for specific pieces of information and advice, using the table of contents or the index.

The book doesn't try to cover every possible kind of group or meeting. Formal procedures in formal meetings, though summarised, are not described in detail. And it contains no academic analysis of organisational cultures or group dynamics: though grounded in research, as well as long personal experience, it's strictly a practical guide to the most common circumstances a chair is likely to experience – whether the setting is a company or co-operative, a public or political body, a charity or community group, or a professional or trade association.

## A note on terminology

Walter Citrine first published his standard guide *The Labour Chairman*, later entitled *The ABC of Chairmanship*, in 1921, and Wal Hannington his *Mr Chairman!* in 1950. The term 'chairman' now seems antiquated, and the more recent term 'chairperson' sounds awkward. Today most people use the term 'chair'. Traditionalists can't criticise it as a new coinage: it was first used in this sense in 1659. 'chair' and 'chairing' are therefore the usages followed in this book. Other terms are in use in some contexts – moderator, speaker, presiding officer, facilitator or president – but chair seems the obvious generic term to prefer.

Chairs may preside over many bodies: boards, committees, task forces, focus groups, assemblies and many more. This guide uses the neutral word 'group' to stand for any of them (except in the special case of a formal 'board' of trustees or directors), and the word 'members' for those who belong to groups.

The term 'secretary' is used for the person who acts as the administrator of a group, typically by organising meetings and taking their minutes. (A company secretary, though, has different and very specific functions.)

## Acknowledgements

I'm grateful to the following people for their invaluable comments on drafts of this book: Sandra Anstey, Alun Burge, Brian Davies, Chris Edwards, R. Brinley Jones, Richard Gibby, David Michael, Chris West and Peter Wakelin. Thanks to Juta Tirona for her quirky cartoons, to Francesca Rhydderch for her expert editing and to Rob Harries of Parthian for all his help. Many thanks also to Phil Spence, who first planted the idea in my mind, and to Carys, Catrin and Elin for all their support.

Material from *The Diaries of a Cabinet Minister: Vol. 3* by Richard Crossman used with kind permission from Penguin.

Material from *A View From the Foothills: The Diaries of Chris Mullin* by Chris Mullin used with kind permission from Profile Books.

Material from *The British Cabinet* by John Mackintosh used with kind permission from Thomson Reuters.

Material from *Man and Superman* by George Bernard Shaw used with kind permission from the Society of Authors, on behalf of the Bernard Shaw Estate.

Although every effort has been made to secure permissions prior to printing this has not always been possible. The publisher apologises for any errors or omissions but if contacted will rectify these at the earliest opportunity.

# 1

## *Does the chair fit?*

## 1.1 Groups and meetings: burden or benefit?

Anyone who spends time in any kind of organisation, commercial or non-commercial, institutional or voluntary, will spend some of that time as a member of a group, very often in meetings. For a few people, at some levels in some organisations, working with groups or in meetings of groups can even prove to be the most common kind of activity.

A group isn't the same thing as a work-group or team. A team, usually under the charge of a single manager or leader, tends to operate as an established set of colleagues within an organisation on a specific range of duties or tasks assigned to it. 'Group' is a wider and looser term. Members of a group, though they share a common purpose, will probably not belong to a single unit in an organisation. They may belong to the same overall body but come together from different units, as in a project group or task force. They may belong to quite different organisations, as in a liaison committee. Or they may represent no one but themselves, like volunteers who join a community group.

What these groups have in common is that they tend to be led by someone who lacks the direct responsibility for some or all of the group's members – typically, a 'chair'. The chair does have status and authority, but not necessarily as the director or manager of the other members of the group. This means that it's not possible for chairs to command a fellow member to take a particular action. Instead, they need to seek consensus, using persuasion and other forms of indirect influence to arrive at agreement and decisions. This makes the nature of the chair's role very different from that of an organisational manager or director.

For many people being a member of a group is a satisfying experience. Working with others towards a common goal, having a chance to make your unique contribution, being valued for your achievements by your peers, interacting with fellow members – all these help to attract people to groups and keep them engaged. A few people aren't by nature group animals. They may just prefer to work on their own. Or they may believe that individual endeavour is usually more productive and efficient than sharing a task with several other people, who could be less expert or hold conflicting views. One reason they give for this belief is that meetings, one of the most common activities of groups, are 'a waste of time'.

It's certainly true that groups tend to hold more meetings than work teams. Their members are not in such frequent contact, and they rely more heavily on discussion and negotiation in order to reach decisions.

Meetings can also soak up huge quantities of time and money. Most office workers spend between four and six hours a week in meetings, and senior managers spend many more. You can buy a 'meeting cost calculator' that will work out the total cost of your meeting. Some surveys report that 50% of meeting time is felt to be irrelevant by those attending, and one found that the total time wasted cost the UK economy £26 billion in 2011.[2] Meetings can become an impediment, rather than an aid, to getting things done. The economist John Kenneth Galbraith spoke for many cynics when he said that 'meetings are a great trap ... they are indispensable when you don't want to do anything',[3] and the US comedian Milton Berle said 'a committee is a group that keeps minutes and loses hours'.

## 1.2 Why have groups? Why hold meetings?
So what are the positive reasons for wanting to form a group or hold a meeting?

The basic principle behind the group, often called the 'synergy' effect, is that individuals together are capable of achieving more than can be done by the same individuals working on their own. This is particularly true when the issues in question are complex and multifaceted, calling not just for different kinds of specialism

---

[2] http://www.newstatesman.com/business/business/2012/05/
wasted-time-meetings-cost-economy-%C2%A326bn-2011
[3] John Kenneth Galbraith, *Ambassador's Journal: A Personal Account of the Kennedy Years*, Boston: Houghton Mifflin, 1969, p.84.

but also for specialists to interact with one another. But there may be other reasons why groups are useful. In some circumstances the agreement of a group is a formal requirement, for example to approve financial accounts. The conclusions of a group, particularly one that is unanimous in its views, may carry much more weight than those of a series of isolated individuals. And regardless of their formal outcomes groups are fruitful ways of sharing experience and knowledge, of teaching and learning, of creating feelings of solidarity and loyalty to a body or an idea, and of course of realising the personal goals of individuals.

What are groups and their meetings used for? In essence they can do one, or both, of two things: they can be used to *explore a subject*, or to *reach a decision*.

*Exploring a subject* can be done independently by each individual member of a group, of course. But a meeting between them is a good way of thinking together and sharing multiple perspectives – of allowing ideas and opinions to touch, collide, prove themselves or even defeat one another. The force of persuasion may cause original views to change under the influence of other speakers. Information can be shared, and evidence and research can be introduced, for example through a presentation or paper by a member, and a space opened for questioning. Different options can be examined, weighed and assessed. The creativity of everyone present can be tapped and pooled. The result may enlighten even if it doesn't bring agreement. And – an important point – those present may leave the meeting feeling that their views have received a fair hearing and that they've had a chance to influence the debate.

*Decision-taking groups and meetings* can take many forms. At one end of the spectrum an emergency group might look at a single urgent problem and try to arrive rapidly at an agreed response. At the other, extensive discussion over a series of meetings could result in a major strategic decision or change of policy. Or the 'decision' may in reality be agreement on recommendations to be passed to a higher authority for ratification or rejection. Again, members should depart feeling that, even if their view has not prevailed, they've played a part in arriving at the decision.

Both kinds of group – exploratory and decision-making – must share a common feature to be successful: their discussions must be *to a purpose*.

The reasons for establishing a group or holding the meeting are likely to be determined in large part by the nature of the body whose members are meeting. The board of trustees of a charitable foundation will meet to make decisions on whether to make grants to applicants. Members of the Planning Committee of a local authority have to decide whether or not to give planning consent to building applications. A company may set up an innovation group to refresh the firm's branding, or government ministers may commission a task-and-finish team to give them advice on a new policy development. In these two cases the group's task is not to decide, but to explore and evaluate possibilities.

Before leaving the reasons for forming groups and holding meetings, we should acknowledge a truth that can work for or against their success. Humans are social and gregarious animals. Groups can provide the opportunity for them not just to 'do business' but to interact in a multitude of complex ways, and from many motivations. These social interactions may have little or nothing to do with the formal reason for their coming together, or their tasks. From the chair's point of view, this can be positive – normal socialisation can help build the group's cohesion and solidarity, and make it work more smoothly. Occasionally, though, it may be negative. Meetings, even quite formal ones, can be undermined by some of the less attractive interactions and behaviours that people bring with them to the group, or form within it: exclusive alliances, suspicions, bickering, cabals, or even vendettas and conspiracies. When this happens the chair needs to be adept at reading the relationships between members, and signs of hidden agendas.

You might say that a central part of the chair's role is to reconcile the individual and the social elements inherent in the group and harness both towards the group's goal.

## 1.3 What's a chair for?

Let's assume, then, that a decision has been taken to set up a group, which will hold meetings. One of the next decisions will often be to identify a chair. But why is a chair needed?

The brief answer is that the chair is the person who has been given the chief responsibility for making a group and its meetings effective. This means everything necessary to give the group the best chance of success: not just the control of discussion, or even the general conduct of the meeting, but everything to do with the group and how it operates.

Some simple groups, especially small and informal ones, may not need someone to organise them and their discussions. In business meetings of the Society of Friends ('Quakers') there is no chair as such. But most meetings do require a chair.

Occasionally people object to the presence of a chair on the grounds that no one should be singled out who might dominate discussion or impose decisions. This, however, is to mistake the true role of the chair. A dominating or domineering chair is a bad chair. The chair might advise, stimulate or steer but should never browbeat or bully or try to override the clear view of the other members. The most common metaphor used for the chair is the captain of the ship, who leads the crew members to a chosen destination, marshalling the seas, the winds and the skills of the mariners. But this is too strong a comparison: the captain, after all, holds absolute power and from time to time will use it. A closer one is the leader of a string quartet. In a quartet, typically self-governing and non-hierarchical, all four performers are completely equal, but they normally designate one of their number as the member who supplies the non-verbal cues, movements of the head or eye, that bring in the other players at the right time. A successful meeting is to some extent a performance, and the adroitness of the chair in co-ordinating its conduct is crucial.

Some groups work with two or more chairs. Sometimes this is an outcome of the nature of the group. For example, the group might be a joint body, containing representatives of two

7

organisations or interests. In the interests of equality its rules might say that it will have two chairs, one from each side, and each chair taking turns to preside over meetings. Or it might be agreed that the chair will rotate among the members of a group, out of respect for egalitarian principles or to give all the members a taste of the experience of occupying the chair. Sharing the chair can often work well, especially in less formal groups or when members are already experienced at chairing in other contexts. But there are dangers, too. Continuity of leadership can sometimes be lost, for example between meetings, when it may be unclear who the responsible person is, and the group can appear to be in limbo. Discussions and decisions need to be recorded and communicated very carefully, to avoid confusion and misunderstanding. There's also more chance of having a less than competent chair.

## 1.4 What skills does a chair need?

It's entirely possible to learn to be an excellent chair. Chairs are not born, but made. That's not to say that people who, for example, can instinctively empathise with the feelings of other people, or who are by nature organised and methodical, don't have an advantage. But in essence the skills of a chair are a set of techniques and behaviours that can be taught and learned.

These are the five main groups of skills and behaviours a good chair should try to master:

* attentiveness
* empathy
* integrity
* acumen
* leadership

*Attentiveness*
After the first hour of a meeting look around the table at your colleagues. How many of them look as though they're paying full attention? Even the most assiduous members of the group can find themselves taking less interest in some parts of a group's

8

work than others. They may let their minds wander, or even be tempted to take a short nap.

For the chair, to 'nod off' is anathema. In general, you should never lose sight of the group and its aims. In meetings, the chair is one of only two people in the room – the other is the secretary – who can't afford to pay anything but their full attention to what's being said throughout the whole meeting. Nothing is more certain to erode your reputation as chair than having to confess that you've just missed the most forceful and intelligent contribution to the discussion.

Alison: ... So that's what I've found from my research over the last few weeks. It puts a completely different complexion on our discussions.

Chair: [waking from a daydream] I'm sorry, Alison, I didn't quite catch what you were saying there. I wonder if you could repeat it?

Alison: Oh, I'm sorry, perhaps I wasn't very clear in the way I explained that. I'll start again ...

[Other members sigh inwardly.]

Staying awake, though, is just the bare minimum. The chair also has to listen especially carefully, to have an 'active' ear. Indeed, active listening is probably the key requirement once discussion has started. Active listening means that you're able to do two things:

• hear, understand and recall what the speaker is saying
• feed back – that is, paraphrase or re-state – what's been said

The second of these, feeding back, is an essential skill if you're going to be successful in clarifying the speaker's views (direct feedback to the speaker), testing them on the other members (feedback to the whole meeting) and preparing to arrive at an agreed decision. If you can prove that you're listening by challenging, paraphrasing and summarising, other members of the group are likely to follow your lead and pay the same attention.

As well as registering *what* is said a good chair will also be paying attention to *how*. Tone of voice, speed of speech, body position, direction of sight: all of these can give clues about what the speaker's intentions are. Sometimes words disguise an unspoken opinion or emotion. So good listening means using your eyes as much as your ears.

You need, too, to be attentive to what *isn't* said, and who *isn't* speaking. There might be several reasons why someone isn't participating in the meeting: lack of expertise, lack of confidence, fear of another member, boredom or hostility. The chair should try to keep an eye open for non-participants, and if necessary, aim to involve them.

Attentiveness is a useful skill outside the meeting, too. In fact it's especially useful then, in order to make sure that the tasks the group has agreed are being completed, or to maintain personal contact with members in order to sustain their interest and commitment.

Being attentive, therefore, extends well beyond just 'keeping your ears open'. It slides into the second set of abilities: empathetic skills.

## Empathy

The work 'empathy' is derived from two Greek words and means 'experiencing as if within' or 'feeling into' another person. It doesn't mean the same thing as 'sympathy', which means 'experiencing with' or 'feeling with' another. To feel or express sympathy requires you only to acknowledge what it is that another other person is suffering: you are concerned for their wellbeing. To be empathetic, on the other hand, is to put yourself in the shoes of others, to share their emotions, to recreate imaginatively what feelings and thoughts they're going through. It's at once a more objective and a more emotionally imaginative process.

10

An empathetic sense is highly useful when chairing a meeting. To be able to get a feel for how people approach a meeting, where they're 'coming from', both intellectually and emotionally, puts a chair in a strong position. It becomes easier to sense whether members have a positive, negative or indifferent attitude to the group, to 'read' what members are saying, and to anticipate how they're likely to react to a controversial proposal.

To work in this way you'll need to cultivate the habit of putting yourself in the place of others – of imagining yourself 'standing in' their mental space. Nature fails to endow some people with this ability, but those who are equipped with empathetic abilities can practise and improve them in all kinds of social contexts, either systematically or simply through the practice of 'living well' with other people. Some contemporary psychologists maintain that empathising is a capability 'wired in' to the female, but not the male, brain.[4] Whether this is true or not, chairs of both sexes should try their best to develop and train their capacity to tune in to the thoughts and feelings of others.

As chair you'll need to get to know the members as people so that you're in a position to empathise with them. This can be hard to do – for example, if the meeting contains a large number of participants, or consists entirely of strangers, or doesn't meet regularly enough for you to develop any real personal knowledge. There are, though, ways of doing the best you can to become familiar with those you're chairing – as people as well as representatives in a meeting. The most obvious is to make sure you keep in contact with individual members of the group outside meetings: it's much easier to develop an understanding of, and feeling for, their position if you take the trouble to communicate with them individually and informally. But even if you encounter people for the first time in the meeting, careful observation may give you clues about their positions.

Feeling empathy, of course, doesn't mean that you're going to

---

[4] For example, Simon Baron-Cohen, *The Essential Difference*, London: Allen Lane, 2003.

take the side of the person whose situation you're considering. Unlike sympathy, empathy is a more objective process and doesn't mean leaving your judgement behind or setting aside your own feelings. It's important that as chair you can combine an understanding of the standpoint of others with an ability to keep your independence and your fairness – in short, your integrity.

## Integrity

Integrity means wholeness, or 'one-ness'. To other people a person with integrity will appear as someone they can always depend on to behave in a consistent way – and not just a consistent way, but a consistently fair and honest way, in accordance with a coherent framework of values and principles.

Integrity is probably the chair's most powerful asset. You may come to the task without the prior benefit of any particular authority, seniority or reputation. But if you can show that you possess – and put to good use – a measure of integrity, then you're likely to command respect and trust from everyone in the group (and many outside it). Almost everything about a meeting – its tone, its operation, its unwritten rules and behaviour – can be influenced for the better by a chair who is seen by all the members as fair, honest, considerate and consistent. People often talk about the 'gravitas' of good chairs: their weight, seriousness and ability to command respect. Integrity and trust lend much more gravitas to a chair than fame or high social standing.

It's hard to overestimate the importance of trust to the chair. According to the philosopher Onora O'Neill, Confucius told his disciple Tsze-kung that three things are needed for government: weapons, food and trust. If a ruler can't hold on to all three, he should give up the weapons first and the food next. Trust should be guarded to the end, for 'without trust we cannot stand'.[5]

---

[5] Onora O'Neill, *A Question of Trust*. (The BBC Reith Lectures 2002), Cambridge: Cambridge UP, 2002, Lecture 1: 'Spreading suspicion'. http://downloads.bbc.co.uk/rmhttp/radio4/transcripts/20020403_ reith.pdf

The key ingredient of integrity is consistency, which in turn is closely connected with two traditional virtues of the chair, namely fairness and impartiality. The maxim 'a chair should never take sides' isn't correct or appropriate in all circumstances. But as a general rule the chair should certainly aim at fairness and impartiality at all times during the course of discussions: in selecting members to speak, in allocating time to different speakers, in summarising opposing arguments, and in many other circumstances.

Treating everyone with equal respect is another, allied attribute of an effective chair. Even if you know or sense that the other members don't regard themselves as equals, you should assume that they are. Avoid having 'favourites', or writing others off as of less value to the task in hand. This isn't always easy to do in practice. It can be tempting to turn almost automatically to the person you believe is likely to provide the most creative or positive contribution to the discussion, especially when time is short. But you should try to resist the temptation. Turn instead to someone who hasn't so far contributed: you may be surprised by what you receive back.

It's something of a balancing act to demonstrate impartiality without being blown in every direction and appearing to be weak and directionless in your chairing. But equally dangerous is to resist being influenced by others and rely only on your own personal instinct. A chair of this kind risks losing touch with others and appearing to be autocratic.

Integrity can also help you out in more difficult situations. For example, if in polarised debates you respond to raised voices and lost tempers by keeping calm, respectful and fair to all, you're likely to restore equanimity more easily and attract the gratitude of everyone present.

## Acumen

Groups and meetings can tackle complex subjects. The subjects can be numerous and varied. Discussion can move rapidly in all directions, or become confused or repetitive. So it's one of the roles of the chair to try to make sense of what's been said and what's been decided.

This calls for the mixture of analytical skills, sense of judgement and quickness of thought that can be summed up in the word 'acumen'. The Latin word acumen means 'sharpness' or 'penetration'. It suggests being able to understand the issues quickly, and to think smartly and clearly, on your feet. In a meeting you'll need to use acumen in two particular contexts: when steering discussion and when summing up discussion in order to bring the meeting to a conclusion.

While listening to all the different voices and views around the table you should be developing a sense of the overall 'drift' of a discussion. What are the key or recurring themes? Is a consensus coalescing around a particular opinion? Or, on the contrary, is opinion split? If so, is the split equal, or are majority and minority views emerging? The ability to answer these questions will depend on how quickly you're able to discern how the discussion is progressing. There are techniques you can use to help you. Two have been mentioned already: listening and watching attentively, and repeating back to the group what you think has been said, to gain a better idea of its significance.

At the end of a discussion, when the time comes to summarise and conclude, you'll need similar presence of mind. Once you've closed the debate the members will be looking to you to weigh up the arguments, based on a fair analysis of the contributions, and to suggest a solution or way forward. Depending on the complexity of the topic and the length of the discussion this could be a relatively simple task – or a seriously challenging one, which may call for a vote to be taken. In both cases, though, penetrating intelligence and quickness of thought are great advantages to any chair.

Rapidity of thought, of course, doesn't mean that you have to be rapid in your judgement of others. Quite the opposite: a good chair is a patient person, slow to show intolerance or anger, slow to turn against troublesome speakers and silence them. Calmness and self-control are useful virtues, and add to the trust others have in you.

## Leadership

From some of what's been said so far it might seem that the role of the chair is simply to 'hold the ring': to moderate the group and take care of the mechanics of the meeting, like the agenda and the order of speakers, and to reflect its collective sense. One writer likens the chair to an air traffic controller: someone who doesn't have responsibility for piloting the plane, only for ensuring the conditions to allow it to take off and land safely.

But only the simplest and most formal of groups can work in this way. Normally the chair must act in many ways, large and small, as a leader rather a follower or a facilitator. All groups have at least one definite goal, and it's the chair who must assume the main responsibility for achieving it. This alone means that leadership is crucial.

Leadership often starts right at the beginning, with the formation of the group. Circumstances vary – often chairs inherit already existing and well-established committees – but sometimes the chair will have a say in the task of the group: who will be its members, its terms of reference, where and how often it will meet, and so on.

Though the secretary will also have a part to play, the chair should be responsible for drawing up or approving the agenda, and, during the meeting itself, for making sure that each agenda item receives its just share of time. Since time in general is so important the chair needs to take care that the meeting doesn't overrun.

Regulating discussion also calls for leadership – to resolve conflict, to avoid some members dominating to the exclusion of others, to give new momentum to a sluggish debate, to discourage repetition, to give a boost to sagging morale, to challenge members if they've neglected an aspect of the subject. In some circumstances (and depending on your powers) you may feel the need to give a strong steer towards a solution – for example, if there's complete deadlock.

15

> Jane: I can't see any way forward. We seem to have looked at every option and thrown them all out.
>
> Tom: I agree. We seem to be wasting our time.
>
> Chair: Yes, it looks like that. But I wonder if we've overlooked something. It would be a pity to report to the Board that we've failed, wouldn't it? Suppose we go round the table and I ask each of you to write on a piece of paper the solution you prefer and one positive reason why. Then we'll pool your ideas, discuss the top choices in more detail and see if we can reach a consensus.
>
> Tom: OK, I'd be happy to give it a go ...
>
> Jane: Yes, that doesn't sound a bad idea.

An effective chair won't hesitate to guide the general direction of the group, for example to propose themes for treatment in the next meeting, and to sustain the 'emotional dynamic', a critical factor in the successful operation of any but the most ephemeral group. In a more permanent group, such as a work team within a single organisation, the chair may have an 'inspiring' role to play, in aiding the group's growth and ability to act as a coherent and creative entity.

And finally, if circumstances call for it, the chair will be the one who acts as the official face of the group, speaking in public or to the media on behalf of all the members, or writing about the group's work. This calls for both leadership and media skills. It's likely to be the chair, too, who represents the group and conveys its decisions to other bodies.

In all these areas you should be able to give shape and direction to a meeting or a group, using sensitivity and tact and without causing the other members to regard you as an autocrat.

Discussions about leadership have a habit of drifting into the question of 'charisma', and how essential or not that quality may be. In chairing, charisma, far from being an advantage, can get in the way of effective groups and meetings. Inevitably a leader with a 'halo' is likely to dominate the room to the exclusion of the views of others. During the Second World War it was noted how meetings of the Cabinet were shorter and more to the point when Winston Churchill was absent and the more modest Deputy Prime Minister, Clement Attlee, presided.

## 1.5 What knowledge does a chair need?

These, then, are the main generic skills a chair needs. What about knowledge of the subjects under discussion? Is a chair expected to be an expert in the field?

Sometimes it's sufficient that the chair has a general working familiarity with the topics under discussion or perhaps a professional background in the field, without necessarily being an expert personally. After all, many of the other members of the group will have been selected because of the expertise and specialities they can bring, and the chair will be able to turn to them for advice at the appropriate time. On the other hand, in other contexts, especially where the organisation is formal, large and has substantial resources, relevant experience could be regarded as essential. After the Co-operative Bank, with assets of £47bn, came close to collapse in 2013, the Chair of the House of Commons Treasury Select Committee reviewing the case came to the conclusion, after cross-examining the lay Chair of the Bank, that 'the chairman of a bank must have a good deal of financial experience and expertise'.

At other times it can be positively helpful for the chair to be a non-expert. Suppose the group's work is going to result in a report that other non-experts will be expected to read and understand. In this case the chair can act as a proxy for the 'innocent reader', asking the expert members to clarify and simplify what they're saying. Ignorance can even be a good position from which to ask for plain language explanations on behalf of other 'innocents' in the group:

Bert:   ... So it looks as though their output diversification
        strategy won't necessarily derisk their underlying
        leveraged asset.
Chair:  I'm sorry, Bert, but for the sake of financial
        numbskulls like me I wonder if you could just explain
        that last bit?
Bert:   Oh, sorry. I meant to say they're so deep in debt they
        may go bust, despite making more varied products.
Jane:   I'm so glad you asked that, Chair!

Even the chair who's an acknowledged 'amateur', though, should
have developed an appreciation of the values and principles of
the group and its area of activity.

### 1.6 What are the chair's functions?

The chair is the person who has the chief responsibility for
making a group effective and its meetings useful. The main
functions of the chair can be summarised simply:

* to make sure that all the relevant matters allocated to the
  group receive fair treatment, in or outside meetings
* to make sure that the group reaches definite and
  understood conclusions, so that it fulfils its objectives

It follows that what an effective chair can contribute are:

* a guarantee of a just and balanced discussion, through
  building evidence and generating options
* an efficient path towards effective decisions, through
  weighing the evidence and judging the options

A third, desirable contribution, especially with long-term groups,
is to build a feeling of well-being, of co-operative travelling
towards a common destination. This doesn't mean that everyone
has to agree on everything – that could hamper healthy debate

and difference – but it should help to maintain people's interest in the group's outcomes, and nurture a sense of ownership of them.

To be more specific, chairs may be expected, or expect themselves, to carry out some or all of these roles:

- establish the group, its remit and membership
- plan agendas and work programmes
- chair meetings of the group, guiding it towards clear decisions
- co-ordinate the contribution of members and assign tasks to them
- supervise and support the chief executive, if one exists
- direct the work of the group's officials, for example the secretary or a researcher
- evaluate the success of the group and its individual members
- convey the results of the group's work, for example in a report
- report to the parent body or officer
- shield the group from exposure to legal, financial or other threats
- represent the group publicly, for example in the media

## 1.7 How do I learn to be a good chair?

There are four main ways of gaining the skills you need to be an effective chair: reading how to do it, being trained (or training yourself) how to do it, observing how to do it and how not to do it – and just doing it. They're not mutually exclusive: you could try all four with benefit. You might also find it useful to seek out a mentor with whom you can share problems and reflect on your experience as it grows.

Reading will give you a basic grounding, but no written guide – even this one! – will be enough on its own. There are numerous training courses offered by organisations and consultants, mainly face-to-face and usually including role-play exercises. Other courses are available in audiovisual and online form. They all have their uses. But the real world is a far better teacher. Observing and doing are likely to prepare you better than the best textbook or course.

If you're a member of any group, try to observe, without neglecting your allotted role in the meeting, how the chair behaves. Watching capable and experienced chairs in action – how they introduce the meeting and involve the members, how they control discussion and manage conflict, how they move towards decisions – will give you an insight into all the critical skills and how to use them. Observing poor chairs can be almost equally illuminating, if you can ignore your frustration and try to work out how you would behave in the same circumstances.

The hardest way to learn is to do the chairing. Being thrown into the chair without any preparation is unenviable and not to be recommended. But if you've had at least some initiation then the first experience of being responsible for a meeting can only offer a host of lessons to the reflective chair. A second and third experience will help further, as will every occasion after that, especially if you make a written or mental note immediately after each meeting of how successful you were. You could also ask a sympathetic participant who was present what went well and what went less well (see section 6.7).

'Initiation' might come not just through the kinds of preparation already mentioned, but also through doing 'trainee' roles in the group, or in another group. Experience of being a group's secretary will give you direct and valuable experience of the administration and paperwork of meetings, including agenda-setting and minute-taking (a crucial and often undervalued skill), as well as the chance to watch the chair in action. An even better observation post is the office of vice-chair or deputy chair. Some organisations explicitly or implicitly regard the vice-chair is an apprenticeship position for a prospective or potential chair.

# 2

## Knowing your role

In this chapter we turn to the role you're likely to play as chair in your particular circumstances. What kind of a chair you're going to be will depend in large part on a combination of factors: how you arrived in the position in the first place; the nature, aims and membership of your group; and the ways in which the group operates and behaves.

## 2.1 How do you get to be chair?

If a body or meeting needs a chair, how is that person selected? There are several possibilities. The chair may be:

- appointed by a higher authority: either by a *body*, like a board or council, or by an *individual*, like a company's chief executive
- self-appointed, for example by being a head of department in an organisation
- elected or agreed by the group itself

The selection decision could be based on one or more criteria, including:

- position or seniority in the organisation
- knowledge or expertise in the field concerned
- experience in chairing or similar skills
- independence from the processes or problems under discussion
- who is available for the task

As for which selection method and criteria will be applied, this will depend on the particular circumstances at the time. All you can say for certain is that the decision is one that shouldn't be taken lightly. A suitable chair will give the group and its meetings a good chance of success. A poorly chosen chair may doom the group to frustration or failure.

Later on, it's worth remembering how you got to be chair, because towards the end of your period, depending on the circumstances, you may find you have a role to play in the choice of your successor.

So here you are, in the chair. Or rather you've just been appointed as chair. What are the questions you should be asking yourself at the beginning, before your first meeting? There are five main groups of issues:

- the context in which you'll be working
- the aims of your group or meeting
- the membership of the group
- how the group will operate
- how the group will behave

## 2.2 The context
The first thing to consider is the context of your position as chair. What's the nature of your group, and what is its responsibility to any parent group?

It's possible that there's no parent organisation: your group might be independent and responsible for its own decisions. This will be true in the case of the board of a charity. Remember, though, that even if it's not a subordinate body your group may be answerable to others in some way. A charity, for example, must abide by charity law and may be supervised by a statutory commission. Where a parent body is lacking the chair will be responsible only to the other members of the group.

Often, though, there will be an external accountability. The group could be a committee of a parent body and entirely dependent upon it, or a taskforce established by an individual company manager. It might be accountable to an external funder. In these cases your task as chair doesn't end with the conclusion of the meeting. You must be bear responsibility for the group's decisions or recommendations. You might be expected to report personally to the appropriate authority, which would have the freedom to alter the task or composition or timetable of your group.

You may find that your group is a 'co-ordination' or 'liaison' committee, and responsible to more than one parent organisation. This is an uncomfortable position to be in, especially when the parents can't agree on what you should do.

Another consideration is duration. Your group may be a semi-permanent one, with a continuing function, like the council of a university or the audit committee of a public body. If so, it's likely to have a series of standard functions and a regular timetable. The agenda may even write itself. There might also be a time limit to the period of the chair.

Other groups are set up with specific tasks and asked to report within specific periods. This gives the chair more scope to choose members and design timetables of meetings and work, but imposes what might be a demanding deadline.

What is your role as chair to be? Again, much will depend on the context. Large or formally constituted bodies, like companies or public boards, will often specify the duties of the chair, in 'articles of association' in the case of companies, or charters, statutes, ordinances or similar documents in the case of public bodies. Other groups may not, and you'll need to rely on a more generic list of the kind described in section 1.6.

Check to see whether your group or you personally have any legal, financial or other responsibilities, and if so be clear about what they are.

Finally, it's worth asking whether there are any special circumstances that affect the role of the chair. For example, public boards will often include the chief executive of the body concerned – probably 'in attendance' rather than as a member. This person will have an important role in determining the business of the meeting, and will be responsible for carrying out the board's decisions. The chief executive and the chair of the board will ideally have a close relationship or 'chemistry' – but not too close, since the former will be formally answerable to the latter. In this case the chair holds a heavy and crucial responsibility outside the context of the meeting. See section 6.3 for more on the relationship between the chair and the chief executive.

## 2.3 The group's aims

The most important question for you to consider to start with is what objectives the group has.

All groups should have an objective, even those that exist to explore a subject with no necessary outcome, or just to expand the consciousness of their members. The statement of aims is often known as the group's 'terms of reference'. The terms of reference should present, as concisely as possible, the scope of the group's responsibilities and the specific objectives set for it. Ideally the objectives should conform to the criteria contained in the well-known 'SMART' formula: specific, measurable, attainable, relevant and time-bound. The terms of reference might be accompanied by other information or instructions, for example about the group's membership and ways of operating, what resources might be available, how to carry out the task, or who to consult while doing so.

**Northsea Council Planning Committee**
**Task Force on Solar Panels: terms of reference**
Cllr Meleri Jones to chair a task force to examine whether and how the Council should support the take-up of solar power in the county.

1   Research and evaluate the effectiveness of intervention by local authorities on  initiatives to increase the use of solar power
2   Collect comparative information on other councils' support for solar power
3   Consult interested groups, firms and the public within the county on their views
4   Report to the Planning Committee with recommendations by the end of June 2015

Members: selected members of the Committee, with co-opted external experts. Planning Department staff to provide research and secretarial assistance.

A self-governing group will be able to devise its own terms of reference. In other cases they may be handed down to the group and the chair by a higher authority. These may be 'tablets of stone', but it's worth enquiring whether the group has the flexibility to suggest changes or extensions that might suggest themselves to members at an early stage. Even better, the authority might be willing for the group to draft its own terms of reference, for subsequent approval.

The value of having a statement of aims is that all the group's members know why the group exists, and can judge later on how close to achieving its objectives it has come. And of course those outside the group will be able to grasp at once what the group is about, and to assess its success or failure against its aims.

As the chair it's worth taking some time to ponder not just the words used in any terms of reference that are given to you, but what might lie behind them. Governments have been known to set up investigatory commissions and remit to them difficult subjects they wish to keep out of the public eye for a few years, and one Westminster cynic once said 'A committee is a cul-de-sac down which ideas are lured and then quietly strangled'. It's unlikely you'll be the victim or willing agent of this kind of manoeuvre, but it pays to be clear-eyed about what is really being expected from your work. Who's commissioned the group? With what intent? Is your task a truly disinterested search for the truth, at one end of the spectrum, or, at the other, designed to justify a decision already tacitly made? Are the people you report to likely to listen to or act on the recommendations your group might make? What clout will your group have? Will people be on tenterhooks to hear your conclusions, or, on the contrary, is there a risk your report will end up as unread 'shelfware'?

If your group is a long-term or permanent one it's worth

revisiting its terms of reference from time to time, in case changes are needed to reflect shifting circumstances.

## 2.4 The group's members

A group is made or broken by its members, so thinking about the people you'll be chairing, or who you'll choose if you have a choice, is well worth taking time over.

There's a basic distinction between people who are paid (or otherwise obliged) to be members of your group, and people who have chosen to be there. If the members are all volunteers you may have less influence over them. They can elect not to go along with your requests or the group's decisions, and will face no sanction for their action, so persuasion will be your main method of achieving your goals.

Let's assume that you have a total or partial choice about who the members will be. How should you do the selecting? The key question to ask is: 'What will be the best collection of people to give us the best chance of achieving the group's aims?' In order to answer it, you need to think about some of the following:

- Who knows most about the subject, or about the group's history or procedure?
- Who has a stake in the likely or possible outcomes?
- Who's likely to make a substantial contribution, rather than adopt a more passive role?
- Who'll offer new or alternative or creative views in discussion?
- Who'll bring useful personal qualities, like a positive outlook or a willingness to work hard?
- Who'll be able to afford the time to be a member and come to meetings?
- Do you need to include people who represent particular constituencies or stakeholders?

There are some traps you'll need to avoid:

- rounding up 'the usual suspects' on the basis of personal acquaintance or past record, and ignoring less obvious candidates for membership
- packing the group with members who think alike or operate in similar ways: this can lead to homogeneity of view ('groupthink') and exclude unorthodox but worthwhile options
- choosing people who 'ought to be there' because of their position or for historical reasons, but who you know will contribute little or nothing to the group, or won't turn up often enough
- keeping the membership too 'tight' by restricting the number of members to a small clique; or the opposite, adding too many members, perhaps out of anxiety about not offending people

One way to avoid these pitfalls is to start with a blank sheet and add possible names, justifying each in turn according to their likely contribution, and at the same time taking care to think about people beyond your normal circles.

There's no such thing as an ideal number of members. Too many people could make meetings more difficult to manage and decisions harder to reach. It could discourage more reserved members from making a full contribution. Some members may become disengaged, and inner groups may form. Too few, on the other hand, and you run the risk of including too narrow a range of expertise and opinion, and of arriving at decisions too easily. A multi-disciplinary case conference, for example, must include all the relevant people, even at the expense of larger-than-ideal numbers. A great deal depends on specific circumstances, but you should be able to find a happy medium – a number that will ensure representation of the right knowledge, skills and interests, without resulting in an unmanageable meeting.

Writers often try to prescribe what would be the ideal mix of member types, based on their suitability for different dynamic roles in the group or the meeting. So, for example, Meredith Belbin specified nine roles needed for an effective group: the Plant, the Resource Investigator, the Coordinator, the Shaper, the Monitor-Evaluator, the Teamworker, the Implementer, the Completer and the Specialist.[6] Most of these complex classifications break down when applied to the real world, but it will do no harm to ponder what different kinds of intellectual strengths you'll need for the task in hand. Many groups would benefit from including, as a minimum, the following characters:

Mel the Method
Pays close attention to detail, keen on evidence and research, keeps the group to its timetable. Unlikely to produce completely new ideas, as Val will.

Val the Vision
Creative imagination, thinks big, generates new ideas, transcends mundane practicalities. Lifts discussion to realms untouched by Mel and Steve.

Steve the Sceptic
Expert analyser, subjects arguments to rigorous scrutiny, keeps Val in check.

There's one remaining aspect of the composition of the group that you'll need to consider carefully: how it reflects the wider membership of the organisation or of the public as a whole; in

---

[6] R. Meredith Belbin, *Management Teams: Why They Succeed or Fail*. Amsterdam: Butterworth-Heinemann, 1981.

other words, its representativeness. For some groups this may be a critical and highly sensitive issue. Ask yourself these questions:

- Do different interest groups need to be represented to legitimise the work of the group?
- Is the gender balance acceptable?
- Is the group ethnically diverse?
- Are other characteristics relevant – disability, educational background, sexual orientation or religion?
- Are there legal or other requirements to be met in these areas?
- Is the group dominated by older people? It can prove difficult to attract young people to committees, despite the learning and development opportunities they offer, whereas older people seem to relish them (retired people, of course, have more spare time for voluntary groups). According to the Charity Commission, in 2010 only 0.5% of charity trustees were aged 18-24, and the mean age of a charity trustee was 57 years.
- Is social diversity present? Are there too few 'ordinary people', or working-class as opposed to middle-class people? The wealthy, titled and well-connected are often over-represented on boards: they're felt to bring credibility, glamour and access to potential donors, rather than the necessary skills and behaviours.

There are several reasons why your group should take representativeness seriously. It may be perceived to lack legitimacy if its composition is skewed towards a particular constituency. You might face a challenge from members of your organisation, your funders, the government or the public. Just as important, you may be missing out on the talent, knowledge and skills available among people unrepresented in your group. This last point is the key to overcoming what might seem on first sight a conflict between appointing members on the basis of their merit and on the basis of their representativeness.

31

When you become chair, however, you may inherit the membership of a settled or standing group, or the group's constitution lays down the membership rules, or the membership consists entirely of representatives appointed by other bodies. In such cases you'll find you have little flexibility in decisions about who you'll be working with. But you could still consider whether or not you have some room for manoeuvre. For example, the rules might let the group elect, or 'co-opt', additional members. This could add fresh blood and new ideas to a group that was 'coasting', or could improve its representativeness. Or, if your period as chair is an extended one and the period of the members is limited, you might find out who is due to retire when, and reflect on who might take their places.

In either situation, whether you've chosen the members or not, there's one action you should try to take, before you hold your first meeting if possible: get to know your members individually. This will make your job much easier from the start. You'll discover something of your colleagues' professional and employment backgrounds, and begin to sense other attributes: their interests and standpoints, their skills and areas of knowledge, and with luck some of their personal characteristics, like their sense of humour. All of this will help you: to know who to turn to for specialist information or advice, to provide a counter-argument to the prevailing view, to lighten a difficult situation with a joke. At the most basic level, it's always an advantage to the chair to be able to use names with ease, rather

---

[7] Richard Crossman, *The Diaries of a Cabinet Minister, Vol.3: Secretary of State for Social Services, 1968–70*, London: Hamish Hamilton, 1977, p.402.

than to rack one's brains in full view of everyone. More seriously, it helps to know what factors motivate members and satisfy their individual goals.

Knowing members personally can help at any stage. If one of them is in difficulties for some reason and it becomes hard for them to contribute to the group, or their behaviour causes problems, it's easier to have a quiet word with them if you've already established some common personal ground.

One particular task that will face you at the start is to make sure that all your members are prepared for the part they will play in the group. With informal local associations this may mean simply having a quick word beforehand. In the case of more formal and legally constituted groups, like public boards, the chair should ensure that everyone is introduced systematically, probably through training sessions arranged by the staff of the organisation, to the legal, financial and administrative implications of membership. This can be a useful bonding experience if the training is organised for everyone at the same time.

Chair:    Welcome, Yvonne, I think you'll enjoy our meetings.
Yvonne:   I've never belonged to this kind of board before – I'm not sure I can be much use. And the other people look so confident.
Chair:    Oh, they won't bite! We're a very friendly bunch. And I'm sure we can benefit from your expertise. Your background's in risk management, am I right?
Yvonne:   Yes, I helped prepare the Council's risk management policy.
Chair:    That's great – and relevant to today's agenda. When we reach the item on the risk register, would you mind if I bring you in to the discussion?
Yvonne:   Yes, if you're quite sure it would be useful.
Chair:    I certainly am!

Later on, try to encourage the members to get to know one another outside the strict confines of the meeting. For example, you could encourage them to attend launches, lectures or social activities organised by the group. This should help to improve mutual understanding and encourage the cohesiveness of the group. Another opportunity arises if you can arrange a more informal 'away day' from time to time, for the group to discuss fundamental issues without the encumbrance of agendas, papers and business transactions.

## 2.5 How the group will operate

With everything else in place, the chair is ready to plan how the group should carry out its work in practice.

Organising a group can take up an unexpected amount of time and require a surprising amount of ingenuity. You may have no choice but that the burden falls on you as chair, but if circumstances allow it's much better to employ or co-opt a first-class organiser to act as secretary to the group. This way you can be sure that the basic functions of the group are in good hands, freeing you to pay attention to its higher-level needs.

These are the most important roles a secretary can perform on behalf of the group:

* contact members and prepare them, for example by arranging induction or training
* help set the agenda and papers for meetings
* co-ordinate diaries to arrange suitable meeting dates
* distribute the agenda and papers to members
* organise meeting venues, refreshments, visits and other details
* take minutes of meetings
* share problems and issues with the chair between meetings

Arranging meeting dates can sometimes be an unexpectedly laborious task, even with the aid of online timetabling tools, particularly if a group's members are extremely busy people.

One of the secretary's distinctive roles, minute-taking, is a skilled task, and one that is often undervalued today. You should always try to ensure that this responsibility is in the hands of someone experienced, who knows how to note the essentials of a discussion and write minutes in a way that will help the group see immediately what's been discussed and decided. It often helps for this person to be someone who's familiar with the ideas the group is discussing. As a minimum, the minutes will record accurately the decisions taken on each item discussed, and any specific 'actions' agreed, with the names of those responsible for them. As chair you'll need to check and approve minutes before they're issued (see section 5.7 for more details).

Once you've worked out the basics of how you think the group should do its work it's usually worth consulting its members in its first meeting, in order to secure their agreement or possibly to adopt ideas that you hadn't thought about beforehand.

## 2.6 How the group will behave

A group doesn't just 'operate', it behaves – as a collection of different individuals coming together, perhaps for the first time, in a common endeavour. How will they interact? In quiet consensus or noisy disagreement? With confidence and assertiveness, or by holding back and expecting the chair to take a lead? Will schisms or cliques develop, or unexpected alliances?

It goes without saying that your group will inevitably consist of very different individuals. Their temperaments and characteristic ways of behaving are bound to have an effect on the whole group. The experienced chair soon learns to recognise the more common types, and how to cope with them (see section 5.2 for some examples).

It's impossible to legislate for the relationships and behaviours of a group's individual members, but the chair should be able to anticipate how a *group's dynamics* can work. A path of how the behaviour of groups develops over time was charted by Bruce Tuckman in 1965 and remains influential. Tuckman identified four successive stages of a group's life: forming, storming, norming and performing. An initial tentative period of defining and establishing relationships ('forming') is followed (as members' self-confidence increases) by a phase of conflict, where different opinions and interests emerge and collide ('storming'). Eventually differences are settled or reconciled in the interests of achieving the wider objective ('norming') and the group is finally able to work productively and in harmony ('performing'). In fact few groups conform to this over-simple model, but it serves to emphasise a feature of group behaviour with which any chair will be familiar: how conflict and its opposite, consensus, can be both productive and dangerous, according to the circumstances that accompany them. Good chairs will encourage the collision of ideas but discourage personal conflict, and will aim for true agreement while challenging consensus that's too easily reached. In other words, they can influence a group's dynamic.

What the Tuckman model fails to highlight is the crucial importance of *trust* in the lifetime of a group. For a group to function at its most effective all the members have to develop a high degree of confidence – in the importance and relevance of the group's task, in the chair and the way the group and its meetings operate, in the good intentions and competence of one another, and in their ability to complete their task. Trust needs to be built – it's unlikely to be fully present at the start – and the chair will have a critical role in building it, by deploying intelligently all the skills outlined in section 1.4.

Another way of looking at how a group behaves is to think about where *power, status and authority* lie within it, and how they emerge. Formally it may appear that the chair has a large measure of all three, but informally they may be distributed around the members. Some people, for example, might command authority because the others recognise that they possess expert knowledge and information of critical importance to the group's work. A member who's a chief executive will usually carry the status associated with that role and the power conferred by the resources that go with it. Other members might lack expertise and hold no formal position, but possess personal authority: the respect they command or their evident ability to talk sense ensures that everyone listens to what they have to say. Conversely, others may lack the confidence to voice their opinion, or tend to defer to more voluble members. These informal centres of strength are not necessarily stable. They can rise or decline during a group's life, as the result of shifts in relationship within the group, victory or defeat in argument. Or by the behaviour of the chair, who often has the capacity to validate or to challenge the position of members who for whatever reason may have a dominating influence on the group – and to encourage those who feel inhibited by their lack of standing.

A third way of analysing how members of a group behave is by studying the *types of verbal contributions* members make to the discussion. 'Interaction process analysis', devised by Robert Freed Bales,[8] uses a classification to code individual interventions as positive or negative, questioning or answering, and task-oriented or emotional. So, a contribution might be labelled as 'shows solidarity', 'shows agreement', 'shows tension' or 'gives suggestions'. Experienced chairs come to sense, without the need for this kind of ethnographic analysis, how Member A habitually tries to offer helpful information or constructive advice, while Member B has a tendency to become antagonistic and negative. They can then intervene to encourage positive behaviour, and defuse or deflect negative behaviour. (Other members, of course, may have the same antennae and the ability to steer discussion into constructive directions: the chair doesn't have to do everything!)

Something that you might notice when monitoring what individual members say, and how they say it, is that the quantity and nature of their contributions can vary according to gender, and possibly other factors. Recent research has shown that women are 25% less likely to speak than men in meetings,

---

[8]Robert Freed Bales, *Interaction Process Analysis: A Method for the Study of Small Groups*. Cambridge, Mass.: Addison-Wesley, 1950.

especially if they're in a minority.[9] Men, on the other hand, may be more prone to interrupt others or to press their ideas more aggressively.

Bales's method has been criticised because it doesn't measure non-verbal signals that members of a group send out in meetings: whether they sit forward or back, where they cast their eyes, whether they hold their bodies in an open or closed way, how still or mobile their hands are. Again, the chair will try to absorb this information, which is all the more valuable for revealing itself through partially unconscious behaviour, to build a picture of how far each member is engaged in the meeting and, if they are, whether with a positive, negative or indifferent attitude.

Sensitive and sensible chairs, therefore, will be aware of these and other aspects of the behaviour of group members. More than that, they'll be prepared to influence the group's internal dynamics and power structures in order to make its operation more effective. Some of the problems that can arise in this area and the ways they can be overcome are explored in more detail in Chapter 5.

---

[9] Christopher F. Karpowitz, Tali Mendelberg and Lee Shaker, 'Gender Inequality in Deliberative Participation', *American Political Science Review*, Vol. 106, 2012, p.533-47.

# 3

# *Planning the meeting*

The meeting is where the chair is most visible, and where the words and decisions of the chair are most influential. So it always pays to put some thought into preparing for all the meetings you'll chair, and especially the initial one. This chapter explains how best to do this, starting with the question of whether a meeting is necessary, and moving on to location, time and environment, drawing up an agenda, communicating with the group's members, and preparing yourself.

### 3.1 Do you need a meeting?

A question chairs seldom ask themselves, but ought to, is: 'Do I need to call a meeting at all?' Not meeting is an option worth considering. Do you need to have a meeting or even a group of people, if there are other ways of achieving what you want? The answer may be 'No.'

For example, you may want just to share information. You could do this in several ways: by sending a memo or email to all concerned, by using the organisation's intranet, by having individual conversations, or through a regular written brief, cascading information through the organisation.

If you want to consult with people, or take the temperature of their opinions on an issue, rather than bring them together physically, consider whether you could contact them electronically or by post, and ask them to complete an online poll or fill in a questionnaire. Sometimes you'll find that the range of opinion generated this way will be wider than in a meeting, where people may feel inhibited from expressing themselves fully.

Even if your intention is to take an important decision you could ask yourself, 'Do I really need a group or a meeting to do this – or would it be better to delegate the decision to an individual colleague whose responsibility it may be to take that decision anyway?'

Even after you've used this filtering process, though, you'll find that a meeting is likely to be the best way of achieving many aims. The only leaders who can afford to dispense with them completely are dictators – and even Hitler and Stalin found it necessary to surround themselves with cabinets and inner circles to advise them and to hold meetings with them.

## 3.2 Place and time

Assuming you've decided your group should meet, your first task is likely to be planning its first meeting. There's a great deal to be said in favour of holding an early face-to-face meeting of any group where the members have never met together before. It gives them an opportunity to start getting to know one another and to develop the sort of co-operative ethos needed to work together over a period toward a common aim.

When, where and how often should meetings be held? The answers will be influenced by the timetable you have and the availability and location of the members. If they're people with busy diaries it may pay to arrange the dates of meetings for a long period ahead, or over the entire period in the case of a time-bound group. Those with family commitments may have particular time constraints. Regularity – setting the same day of the week, or the same intervals between meetings – may help members plan their diaries, and remember to attend.

Perhaps you won't need, or aren't able, to come together physically on all occasions. If so, you'll need to plan how you're going to get your group together remotely, by phone, email, desktop video, phone conference, videoconference or other means (see section 7.9 for more details).

## 3.3 Duration

Think too about the length of your meetings. It's not always easy to estimate how long they should last. In general, they should be long enough to ensure that discussion isn't stifled, but not so long as to try the patience or mental stamina of the participants. Early experience will usually indicate whether you can adapt times in future meetings. What you do need to avoid is setting arbitrary times that are either too long – Parkinson's Law suggests that business tends to expand to fill the time available for it, and there's nothing more frustrating than 'filling in' unneeded time –

or too short. The newspaper editor William Rees-Mogg had a habit as chair of setting an extremely tight time limit and insisting that the meeting didn't last a minute longer – even if that meant curtailing essential discussion.

Chair:   Good morning everyone! These meetings usually last for an hour and a half, but our agenda looks short, and I can't see much that's of huge importance. Shall we see if we can finish within twenty minutes?

Victor:  Oh, I did hope, Chair, that we could have a thorough debate about losing two of the car parking spaces. Could I raise it under 'Any other business'? I've got a short paper on the subject.

Bethan: Victor, you can't be serious. Car parking? Anyway, 'Any other business' isn't on the agenda.

Others: [general agreement with Bethan]

Chair:   I'm sorry, Victor, the meeting's against you on this one. Come and see me afterwards, if you have time. Now, down to business ...

There are some settings where meeting time seems completely elastic, the outstanding example being universities. In Malcolm Bradbury's campus novel *The History Man* (1975) the sociology lecturers in the University of Watermouth, who are of course 'sophisticates of meetings', begin their 'encounter' at two o'clock, are still on agenda item 1 at three o'clock, and complain bitterly when the long-suffering chair, Professor Marvin, attempts to bring discussions to a close at five-thirty.

It's worth bearing in mind that most people's attention spans can be quite short. If you need every member of your group to give their full concentration to a subject, especially an abstruse one, try not to extend the discussion much beyond thirty minutes. Not every part of the meeting, though, will require the same degree of close attention by everyone, and as long as you craft the agenda well, and build in enough breaks, you should be able to meet over several hours without exhausting yourself and others. Some authorities insist that all meetings should be short meetings, but occasionally a lengthier one is a good idea – for example, to make it worthwhile for those members who've made a long journey to attend.

When preparing the agenda you might think about items not just in terms of their importance or urgency but also in terms of how much mental effort and concentration they're likely to require of your members.

## 3.4 The agenda

Your second critical task, probably in conjunction with the secretary, is to determine the agenda of the meeting – that is, the list of subjects you're going to deal with. Every meeting needs an agenda.

The word 'agenda' is a Latin plural and can be translated in two ways: as 'things that need to be done' and 'things that need to be discussed' – an ambiguity that usefully links discussion with action and practical outcomes. The root meaning of the Latin verb 'agere' is to 'drive forward': a useful motto for any chair. An individual item on an agenda is sometimes called an 'agendum'.

The ambiguity between 'doing' and 'discussing' is important. Matters on an agenda should be there for a purpose. But there can be more than one purpose. In fact there are three distinct types of matter:

- matters for information and noting
- matters for discussion
- matters for discussion *and decision*

Everyone, including the chair, needs to be clear before the meeting about which type each individual item on the agenda belongs to.

Many chairs undervalue the importance of agendas and don't

pay enough attention to getting them right. But a well-crafted agenda is crucial, in several ways:

- it specifies exactly when and where the meeting will be held, and possibly who's expected to be present
- it states clearly what are the main subjects for discussion
- it may suggest what relative weight is attached to different subjects
- it says what members are invited to do (to note or receive, to discuss, or to approve, agree or decide)
- it indicates what papers or other prior information members will need to digest and bring with them

Let's take a specimen agenda and see how and why it's been put together:

**Tideswell Community School Parents' Association**

Members of the Parents' Association Committee are invited to a meeting on 23 September 2014 from 7:00pm to 8:30pm in the School Meeting Room.

Attending: Jean Walsh (Chair), Alun Edwards (Secretary), Teresa Jones (Treasurer), Bob Fisher, Ahmed Faisal, JoJo Holliday, Barbara Smart; Helen Adibojo (Headteacher)

Apologies received from: Nahum Stewart

Agenda
1  Welcome, introductions and apologies
2  Declarations of interest
3  Minutes of last meeting
   *To confirm the minutes of the meeting held on 7 February*
4  Matters arising from the minutes
   *To consider actions and other matters arising from the minutes and not on the agenda, in particular*:
   4.1 Repaving the school drive (Min. 4)

4.2 Sponsorship for the trip to France (Min. 6)
5   Headteacher's report
    *To receive and discuss an oral report from Helen on school developments.*
6   Financial matters (Teresa)
    6.1 Appeal
    *To plan the Association's appeal to raise funds for new equipment*
    6.2 Bank
    *To approve a change of banker for the Association* (Paper PA312)
7   Online learning (Bob)
    *To discuss and take decisions on the recommendations in Bob's paper on the use of tablets in the classroom\ (Paper PA313). Thirty minutes allotted for this item.*
8   Any other business
9   Date of next meeting
    *To note the date of the next meeting (10 February 2015), already agreed.*

The first thing to notice is that this agenda is fairly short: a total of nine items is unlikely to induce 'that sinking feeling' in the people receiving it. Try to confine agendas to no more than ten to fifteen items, and avoid going on to a second page!

The name of the body and when and where the meeting will happen are clearly stated.

It's useful to say when the meeting will end, so that members can make their own plans with certainty. (This meeting lasts an hour and a half – ideally, the maximum length of this kind of business meeting.) If members are likely to be uncertain about a more remote or obscure location, include a map or directions and a postcode (to help those using satnav).

If possible include the names and positions of those who should be at the meeting, and who has already sent apologies for their absence: this is especially useful for new members who are still finding their bearings in the group.

Individual agenda items are numbered and given headings. There's also an indication, in italics, of how precisely the meeting is intended to treat the subject (usually, to note, to discuss or to decide). This is important: members reading the agenda should be completely clear about why an item is there and how they're supposed to approach it. It's good practice to use an active verb ('approve') to make it clear exactly what should happen, and to name the 'owner' of each item: normally this person will introduce the discussion about it.

To expand on the individual agenda items:

1  The chair will usually wish to welcome everyone, especially any new members, note any apologies for absence and make any other introductory remarks that might be needed.
2  This item gives members an opportunity to state whether they have an interest, financial or otherwise, in any of the business to be discussed. Any declaration will be recorded in the minutes of the meeting.
3  Unless there's a good reason to promote another item, it's usual to take next the accuracy of the draft minutes of the last meeting. This may appear to be a formality, but it gives members a chance to disagree with the wording.
4  'Matters arising' then follows naturally. It's an opportunity to report new developments or the results of actions agreed, and to raise queries about uncertainties. In the meeting members may pick up any item from the minutes, but the chair will concentrate on those with associated 'action points'. In the agenda it's often useful to flag items of particular importance, like the two here, but it's best to avoid adding too many. Matters of cardinal importance should be lifted out of 'Matters arising' to form substantive items later in the agenda.

Occasionally 'Matters arising' is placed towards the end of the agenda, so that the meeting can move straight to the substantive items, but usually it's more natural to get the 'leftovers' of the previous meeting out of the way as early as possible.

See section 4.4 for more on Minutes and Matters arising.

5  Meetings often contain reports, to be either noted or discussed. They may be written or, as here, oral. The agenda notes specifically that the Head's report will be oral, and that it's not just for 'noting': it may lead to discussion by the members (see section 4.6 for more on reports).

6  It's good practice to cluster together on the agenda items of the same general type, like the two here, which are both financial in nature and both introduced by the same person, the treasurer. Note that one of the items has an associated paper, to be distributed in advance along with the agenda (see section 4.5 for more on papers).

7  This discussion is clearly signposted, through the indication of time length, as the most important of the evening. Some agendas try to specify timings for all items, though this can have the effect of setting arbitrary and undesirable limits to discussions. There's an associated paper the members are expected to read beforehand.

8  'Any other business' allows members to raise relevant matters not included on the agenda as separate items (see section 4.7 for more details).

9  If the meeting is one of a series it's always helpful to remind members of the date of the next meeting – even if that date has already been decided.

Typically the agenda is agreed by the chair and the secretary, although it's also good practice for the chair to invite all members to suggest items for inclusion (well before the meeting, in order to give plenty of notice).

Some experts recommend that 'meaty' items should be placed

in the middle of the agenda, on the grounds that this is likely to coincide with the point in the meeting when participants are at the peak of their alertness. An unscrupulous chair might place a contentious item towards the end of the agenda, in the expectation that members will be too tired or short of time to give it fair attention.

| | |
|---|---|
| Chair: | Angela, I'm a bit worried about this item on the rent increases. |
| Secretary: | Well, there's certainly likely to be some strong opposition to the proposal. |
| Chair: | Would be best to move it to lower down on the agenda, say to item 12? By that time it will be five thirty and everyone will want to go home. No one will have the energy for a fight, and some of the troublemakers might have left anyway by then. |
| Secretary: | Do you think that's wise? Isn't it better to have the arguments now, rather than store up trouble for another time? Some of them might think we're not being quite honest. |
| Chair: | I suppose you're right, Angela. Let's leave it where it is. |

## 3.5 Communicating with the members

Once the agenda and papers are ready the chair will arrange, often through the secretary, for them to be distributed to members, along with any other information that might be necessary. With luck this will not be too daunting a package for the members to receive. Some formal meetings are presented with hundreds of pages of documentation – reports, discussion documents, papers and minutes of sub-bodies – that make it difficult to identify what are the truly important items of business. If members start complaining about paper mountains you know it's time to change the arrangements.

It's helpful, especially in formal meetings, if papers conform to a standard format and house-style. Each paper should bear its author's name and the date of its completion. It should state what the paper's purpose is, and what the meeting is being asked to do, for example, either to note its contents, or agree to its recommendations. Throughout it should be concise, easy to digest and refer to, and written in accessible language.

When should the agenda and papers be sent out? As a rule of thumb, about a week before the date of the meeting. But it really depends on the circumstances: the important thing is that they don't go out so early that the members have lost them or forgotten about their contents by the time of the meeting, or so late that they have little or no chance of reading them and thinking about how to react to them. In more formal boards there's often a procedural rule that papers must be sent at least a week in advance. It's always best if all the documents go out in a single package, not in confusing dribs and drabs over several days.

How should the agenda and papers be distributed? In the past there was no question: by paper, through the external or internal post. Today there are electronic alternatives: using email with attachments, or a store – a common internal file-store or a document-sharing service hosted in the 'cloud' – from which members can draw down the documents for themselves. These alternatives are attractive, since they save printing costs and allow members to call up the documents directly on their laptops or tablets in the meeting – but they depend on all or most of the members being able to dispense with paper: it's unfair to expect members to bear the cost of printing long documents. If you do rely on electronic documents it helps to distribute 'uneditable' versions (for example in 'PDF' format), so that you can be sure that everyone's working from exactly the same version. Make sure that it's easy to identify papers, and tie them in to agenda items through a simple numbering system.

There are some circumstances where paper is best, even if all members are fully 'electronic'. If, for example, you expect them to read carefully through numerous grant applications, comparing and scoring them, you should send them a full paper set of the papers.

Some members may well have lost their papers or come without them, so it's wise to have a spare set or two to hand at the start of the meeting.

## 3.6 Preparing the environment

The day of the meeting is not far off: it's time for you to think about where it's going to take place, and the practical details of its surroundings. The secretary may be able to take care of the details, but as chair you'll need to be sure that they're all in place.

There are some obvious physiological considerations: how to make the members feel comfortable and able to hear and contribute to discussions easily. Ask yourself these questions:

• At what time of day will the meeting take place? Some writers maintain that late morning is when most people are most mentally alert and most inclined to listen and contribute to discussion. If the meeting has to be late in the day you may have to work harder to avoid people's attention wandering.

• Is the room going to be appropriate for the meeting? Clearly it must be big enough to accommodate everyone, but too large a room can also feel uncomfortable. Above all you need a space that's quiet, without building works outside or people passing through. Are access arrangements and other facilities suitable for any disabled members?

• Are the temperature and ventilation satisfactory? A hot, humid and airless atmosphere can neutralise even the most energising and entertaining chair. It should be possible to adjust temperature and airflow to suit most people present.

• What are the acoustics of the room like? Will everyone be able to hear? Ideally you need a space where sounds neither bounce around too much nor get lost in soft furnishings. In big meetings, will you and other speakers need a microphone?

- Are the seating arrangements suitable for your needs? Seats should be comfortable, without perhaps being over-comfortable, and close but not too close to one another. Some chairs of a puritanical disposition disallow seats and make members stand, in the interests of brevity. Since the time of Queen Victoria members of the Privy Council have traditionally stood at meetings in the presence of the monarch. 'Stand-ups' have their uses, for daily 'status updates' in companies for example, but they're not recommended for lengthier meetings, and of course may discriminate against people who are unable to stand for any period of time.

- And the table? Sometimes it's good to do without one, for example if you want to encourage a creative, open-ended conversation without the distraction of papers and laptops. The arrangement of the tables is worth some thought, since it can affect the attitude and engagement of participants. They may be organised in a circular, horseshoe or rectangular formation, or may be in theatre or cabaret style, or may be configurable to different formations within the same session. Each format has its merits, depending on the circumstances. In most small meetings a table large enough to seat everyone is best – if possible, a round or oval-shaped one, so that everyone can see everyone else without difficulty. As chair you should be able to see all the members without contorting yourself.

- Is suitable equipment available? People's potential needs are now numerous, so this can be a complex question. Will members need badges on their person or name cards on the table in front of them? Are there facilities for image projection (laptop, projector and screen) and for graphics (flipcharts, pens and pencils)? Is an internet connection required, for projection or for individual members' use? If so, how fast does it need to be? Are there enough electrical sockets for members to recharge their laptops, tablets or smartphones? Will you need a simultaneous translator and associated equipment? Facilities for those with special hearing or visual needs? You'll require recording equipment if you need a verbatim record of the meeting.

- Are toilets nearby, and easy to get to? Are water and glasses on the table (essential for a meeting of any length)? Will you need refreshments during breaks, and if so who's going to provide them, and when? A sandwich lunch, or just coffee, tea and biscuits? (A survey by Holiday Inn in 2008 found that 80% of 1,000 UK business professionals polled claimed that biscuits improved the quality and outcome of a meeting.)

## 3.7 Preparing yourself

Last but not least, it's essential that you prepare yourself well for the meeting. *It's hard to overestimate this point.* If you're as ready as you can be, you give yourself an excellent chance of being able to manage anything the meeting might throw at you. If, on the other hand, you're underprepared or you've not done any homework, the other members will find you out and some of your authority will quickly evaporate.

So, refresh your memory about the agenda, and reread any papers accompanying it. Look through the minutes and make a marginal note of any matters you want to raise. Make sure you can answer any queries about each point that might arise, or at least know who to turn to for an expert response. Think about how you're going to introduce the meeting and each individual item. If guests are joining the meeting to speak to members, how are you going to welcome and introduce them? Can you predict any difficulties, any issues that are likely to prove controversial? If so, can you anticipate how you might see your way through them? In very complex cases you may wish to contact relevant people beforehand, to be sure that you've got the full picture, or to take advice on how to handle a predictable dispute. You might ask someone to be prepared to speak on a particular issue.

If you've made this kind of preparation, don't be surprised to find that your copy of the agenda is full of scrawled notes to yourself.

Above all, try to answer the crucial question: 'What do I want us to get out of this discussion?' This isn't to suggest that you should intend always to have a specific outcome in mind, much less that you're planning, as a student of Machiavelli, to manipulate every discussion to produce your predetermined outcome. You might indeed have a preferred result, but on many questions you may be agnostic or even indifferent. It does mean that you should usually take a view beforehand about which of the discussions should result in a firm decision. Your job is to steer the group in such a way that it's able to arrive at the best achievable outcome. You should be able to imagine yourself saying, at the end of the meeting, 'Thank you all very much. We've had an excellent discussion, and because of the decisions we've taken we've moved ahead substantially towards our overall goal.' Not every meeting will in fact end like this, but it's an objective worth aiming for.

This kind of anticipatory thinking is especially valuable in the case of difficult issues. Here are some of the questions you might ask yourself:

- What's the solution I feel would be ideal?
- If that isn't achievable, is there a possible fall-back position that would be acceptable?
- If no agreement is likely to be reached, can treatment of the problem be postponed or dealt with in another way?
- If so, how?

Think, too, about the different members of your group and how they're likely to react to the matters on the agenda:

- Can you expect serious conflicts to come to the surface?
- If so, how do you think you'll deal with them?
- What if the opposite happens, and discussion fails to take

off? How will you spark a discussion that does justice to the issues?

- Do you have the right expertise and knowledge available among those present, and might you find yourself delaying a discussion or decision if they're absent?

Remember, too, that you should be familiar with the basic facts of the group: its terms of reference, its constitution or rules and its membership. At the very least you should be able to refer to these details quickly in the meeting, even if they're not in your head.

Once you've done all this preparatory thinking you could consider what chairing style you're going to adopt in the meeting, to suit the group and the subjects to be covered. You could assume different styles depending on the context. One writer makes a useful distinction between three different styles: *executive*, for mundane business that can be dealt with quickly, *relaxed*, when the pace can be slower and the discussion more exploratory, and *eductive*, when you need to draw as many ideas as possible from all the members.[10]

Now you should be ready for your first meeting of the group.

---

[10] Howell Parry, *Meetings*, London: Croner, 1991, p. 35.

# 4

## *Conducting the meeting, 1: mechanics*

At last we come to the meeting itself and how you're going to conduct it as chair. This chapter deals with some of the good habits that you should cultivate, and some of the standard practices you should be familiar with as you approach and preside over the meeting.

## 4.1 Before the meeting starts

The time when members gather in the room before a meeting, though it might appear inconsequential, is actually quite important. For members who haven't met before it's a chance to get to know one another, and for everyone the informal conversational exchanges may help to develop a sense of friendliness and even solidarity and common purpose. For the chair there are two practical rules worth observing.

*First, arrive early.*
This may sound an obvious piece of advice. But think about the consequences of turning up late. You're flustered and out of breath. Your papers are out of order. The other members wait, patiently or in exasperation, while you arrange yourself. It will hardly make sense for you to start with the words 'Welcome to the meeting', since it's you who's being welcomed to the room. Better to apologise and make a mental note to yourself to do better next time.

Reaching the room before all or most of the members, on the other hand, gives you several advantages. You can organise both your papers and your mind at leisure. You can check the seating, equipment and other practical arrangements, and coordinate business with the secretary. Over coffee you can give a personal welcome to new members or special guests, and generally engender the kind of informal atmosphere you may prefer.

Idiosyncratic chairs use this waiting time in other ways. For example, in a small but regular meeting, they might make sure they sit in a different position at the table from the last time – the intention being to make sure that the other members don't fall into an over-comfortable pattern of seating, and maybe thinking. Suspicious chairs might position the people they think may cause them most trouble directly opposite, or very close to them. And sensible chairs will make sure that the secretary and other essential members sit at their right or left hand for easy communication during the meeting.

*Second, when you start, start on time.*
This too may seem to be hardly worth saying. Of course delays are sometimes inevitable: a key speaker may appear late, or the video link may fail. But if there isn't any good reason to start promptly, do so. One specific reason for this is to encourage the other members to be prompt themselves – not to feel that they have a licence to arrive whenever they like after the start time. More generally, to begin a meeting on time is a sign that the chair is intent on taking time and timekeeping seriously. A few members may chafe at the initial discipline, but later everyone will thank a clock-watching chair for preventing meetings from swelling into exhausting marathons.

## 4.2 Introducing the meeting
The first few minutes can set the tone for the whole meeting. This means that the chair, who normally holds the floor at this point and has everyone's full attention, enjoys an opportunity not only to give specific guidance and information but also to convey less tangible messages, for example about the degree of formality of the discussion. In a mundane annual general meeting, which most people present are usually anxious to see end as quickly as possible, you might want gently to discourage pedants from prolonging discussion unnecessarily, for example by referring playfully to the buffet lunch awaiting everyone outside.

Make sure, though, that you don't allow yourself the luxury of a long speech that will eat into the business of the meeting and exasperate the members.

Ministers' meeting. The first 29 minutes – I timed him – were occupied by a monologue from JP [John Prescott]. Mercifully he was interrupted by a fire alarm about halfway through which brought some light relief, but he paused only to swear at the disembodied voice, and then ploughed on regardless. Gus Macdonald just stared blankly at the table. Keith Hill sat with his eyes raised to heaven, occasionally pulling a face to which I dared not respond since I was in JP's direct line of fire.
*Chris Mullin MP, in his diary, 30 November 1999*[11]

Your first words will usually be to welcome the members. This is often perfunctory, but it does no harm to acknowledge the efforts people have made to come, for example, in travelling from afar. Now is a good time to add less formal comments, so as to put people at ease and sugar the pill of the hard business to come. Some chairs will risk a joke or an anecdote, and some have been known to recite a brief (apposite or comic) poem – but don't attempt humour if you suspect it may fall flat.

If this is the group's first meeting you'll need to summarise its main objectives so that everyone's quite clear about what's expected of them. Outline how you see the group doing its work – the pattern of meetings, the timetable for the different tasks involved, any sub-groups that might be set up, special roles for specific individuals, and so on – and invite the members to give their views and propose any improvements.

It makes sense, too, in an initial meeting, to ask the members to introduce themselves briefly, even if informal introductions have been made before the start. You might ask them to state their title or role, or which body they represent, and something less formal, such as what they hope to derive from contributing to the meeting. Beware, though, that this doesn't take too long. In later meetings you'll need to introduce any new members or

---

[11] Chris Mullin, *A View from the Foothills: The Diaries of Chris Mullin*, edited by Ruth Winstone, London: Profile, 2009, p.52.

guests, and decide whether or not for their sakes to go round the table again with individual introductions.

You'll also need to announce the names of absentees, to be recorded in the minutes. After the meeting you might wish to contact them to give them your own update on what transpired, rather than have them rely on the minutes, when those are distributed later.

Make sure you've a list of essential practicalities to tell the members about: things like the location of toilets, evacuation procedures, and coffee, tea and meal times. If necessary outlaw mobile phone conversations – though nowadays you can hardly ban members from using their laptops, tablets or smart phones, which is where they may keep their papers for the meeting (sometimes it can even help discussion if a factual matter in dispute can be settled straight-away through an internet search). You could issue a stern warning, though, that members shouldn't use their devices to flirt via email, exchange pictures of humorous pets, or indulge in other extraneous activity.

Ask everyone if they have copies of the agenda and all the papers for the meeting in front of them, either on paper or in electronic form. Unless your agenda is very standardised or formal you might ask the members whether they're happy with it as it stands. This gives them a chance to suggest any important additional (unforeseen) item, to flag a minor topic to be raised later under 'Any other business', or to comment on the order of agenda items. The final word on whether to accept such suggestions lies with you.

As for the business on the agenda, it's often helpful to give the members a brief picture of the purpose and likely direction of the meeting as you see them: what are the main objectives you think should have been achieved by the end, which are the crucial subjects for discussion, how this meeting fits in to the group's overall aims, and the likely timetable for discussion of key items.

Chair: A warm welcome to everyone! This is our second meeting. Last time, we introduced ourselves, agreed our terms of reference, and decided how we'd operate. We'll review all that when we look at the minutes in a moment. This time I'd like us to devote most of our time to item 3 on the agenda, the review of children's services. By the end of the discussion I hope we'll have agreed on its aims, content and timetable. Then we can deal more briefly with the other subjects. Does that sound sensible to everyone? Can I just check that you've got all the papers we sent out? Has anyone got any questions or comments before we start?

## 4.3 Timing and the agenda

The meeting proper begins. From the start the chair should have a constant awareness of time passing. It helps (others as well as you) to have your watch in front of you to remind you of the inexorable march of time, and as a warning. It's usually inadvisable to note timings against each item on the agenda, but it doesn't harm to keep a rough timetable in your head of how long you think each will take, and to continue weighing remaining items against remaining time as you go along.

Assuming the timings of agenda items will be somewhat flexible, the question arises, how flexible? Experience and the circumstances of the meeting will usually dictate the answer. The only general rule is that you should try to prevent what you regard as less important matters from absorbing disproportionate quantities of time, and conversely you should seek to reserve enough time for discussion of more important subjects. There are few aspects of a chair's performance that betray clearer signs of incompetence or inexperience than failing to achieve this balance. Chairs usually learn to read the telltale signs that minutiae in the minutes are about to balloon into full-scale debates, with everyone in the room chipping in their opinion. The topic is usually one that anyone can have an expert opinion on. In university or school committees mention of car parking should immediately sound an alarm bell in the chair's head. In local government it may be paper recycling; in a company, the colour of carpets; in a hospital, smoking in the car parks. Trivia have the capacity to run away with your meeting and ruin your reputation as an effective chair. You shouldn't hesitate to end such discussions when they threaten to get out of hand. Remind members that weightier matters await their attention, or suggest they can continue the discussion informally outside the meeting.

## 4.4 Standard agenda items, 1: minutes and matters arising

Meetings vary in format, but most agendas contain some standard features, which all chairs will become familiar with. Perhaps the most common are 'Minutes' and 'Matters arising'. They normally appear as items at or near the beginning of the agenda, so that the group can deal with 'loose ends' from the past before moving on to the present and future.

'Minutes' are simply a summary of what took place in the previous meeting. Minute writing is a specialist skill, and a chair will always be thankful to a secretary who has the ability to produce an accurate, factual and concise account of a meeting. Often minutes record only decisions, with a note of 'actions' for the future and who'll be responsible for executing them. But occasionally it's useful for the secretary to give an outline of the arguments underlying the decisions, especially if you anticipate that in the future there may be a need to refer back to the minutes to remind people exactly why some decisions were reached.

In the meeting it's always best to keep consideration of the accuracy of the minutes ('Minutes') quite separate from discussion of their content ('Matters arising'). Unless you do this, confusion can easily arise in discussion about whether the group is talking about the wording of the minute or its subject. The normal way of avoiding this is to specify them as two separate items on the agenda.

Chair: Are there any corrections to be made to the minutes of
the last meeting?
Ben: In minute 2.4 the name should be Peter 'Clarke', not
'Clark'.
Chair: Thanks, Ben. Any others?
Rana: On minute 5, I've seen Peter since our last meeting: he
said he wasn't able to help us because ...
Chair: Thanks, Rana, but let's stick to the accuracy of the
minutes for now. Could you give us your update under
'Matters arising'?

If your secretary has done a good job there should be few
problems about the accuracy of the minutes and no need for any
discussion, unless members differ in their recollection of a matter
of importance. The secretary should record any corrections,
textual or substantive, in the minutes of the current meeting. If
you need to, confer with the secretary to ensure that the wording
has been captured accurately.

One way of reducing the risk of extended discussion is to
accompany the draft minutes, when they're sent out to members,
with a request for comments to be sent in advance of the
meeting.

The important point about 'Matters arising' is that they enable
you to chase actions that were agreed at the last meeting, and
make sure that they're in hand.

'Matters arising' may take more time than the Minutes. But
they shouldn't take too long. If after half an hour you're still
entangled in the residue of the last meeting there's a danger that
the group's members may lose morale and begin to feel
frustrated. The key is to avoid discussion drifting beyond the
only two functions of 'Matters arising': to review the actions
agreed at the last meeting and to update the group with any
relevant developments on issues originating in the minutes that
don't appear elsewhere on the agenda. It helps if you've prepared
beforehand, by noting particularly important matters arising, and

by reading the minutes carefully and make marginal notes to yourself. During the meeting try to keep updates you or other members give to a minimum length, keep discussion on as tight a rein as you can without stifling debate, and call a halt when discussion threatens to encroach on items you'll be talking about later on. If it looks as though one of the matters arising can't easily be confined to a brief discussion don't be afraid to rule that it will be dealt with later on as an additional agenda item in its own right, or even postponed till the next meeting to allow for a fuller debate and a period of reflection or evidence-gathering in the meantime.

## 4.5 Standard agenda items, 2: papers and presentations

Another common feature of meetings is the paper. A paper opens a subject for consideration or makes a series of proposals, usually as the prelude to an extended discussion and possibly decisions. Alternatively, or in tandem, the group may listen to a personal presentation, with or without audiovisual aids, by a fellow member of the group or by an invited guest.

The paper should have been distributed to members in advance, with the agenda, for them to read and consider before the meeting. If so, the chair should take it that all members have studied its contents carefully and have come to the meeting with their responses mentally prepared. Of course it may be that one or two of them, for good or bad reasons, have failed to do so, but to reprise the document page by page in the meeting not only wastes time but also rewards the negligent and penalises the diligent.

However, it's almost always good practice to preface discussion with a brief introduction summarising the paper, or, better still, drawing out themes that are critical or particularly merit debate. This can help to give a structure to the discussion that will follow and avoid any initial silence as people wonder where to begin. If the paper's author is present, either as a group member or as an external guest, you should invite them to speak, introducing them if necessary and diplomatically warning them not to take long. If the author isn't present it falls to the chair to provide the preface.

Chair: Now we come to item 6. Welcome, Walter, to the
committee, and thank you very much for your paper.
It's very clear and concise, and raises important issues.
Everyone here has read it, but perhaps you'd like to
spend five minutes outlining what you see as the
critical points and what you think we should do? Then
we'll throw the discussion open for ten minutes or so.
(You've made three recommendations in section 5, so
we'll concentrate on those.) Walter, over to you ...

Presentations, although they take up extra time in the meeting,
carry some advantages over a paper on its own. They give
presenters an opportunity to select or reinforce points they
particularly want to make. If well delivered they can make a
stronger and more direct impact on their audience than a written
paper, and they can provide a useful 'change of gear' for the
dynamic of the meeting. And they can stimulate questions and
comments that will emerge immediately and naturally in the
following debate. What you need to do as chair, apart from
making sure that any equipment or other facilities are working,
is to keep the presentation within the time limit, and to be clear
about whether you or the presenter is going to preside over the
ensuing discussion. Tell presenters beforehand how much time
is available to them, and pass them a reminder if there's a danger
of over-running.

At the end the chair needs to summarise what actions, if any,
have been agreed following discussion of the paper or
presentation.

### 4.6 Standard agenda items, 3: reports
Meetings often receive reports. These may come from within your
organisation and its officers – the treasurer, for example, or an
audit committee or other subordinate body answerable to your
group. Or they may come from other bodies, or from your
organisation's representatives on other bodies.

Reporting of this kind, whether on paper or oral, can often seem formulaic and unproductive – a monologue or series of monologues, without definite outcomes and with only desultory questioning or discussion. It can even be a chance for some members to switch off for a time. Only the more numerate and economically aware, for example, may be willing to scrutinise and offer their comments on a financial report.

The best tactic a chair can adopt is to ask for brief reports – reports rather than minutes, if possible – to be submitted beforehand, so that members can scan them before the meeting, with an even briefer oral summary during the meeting highlighting the issues most pertinent to the group's work. Members then have the best chance of approving the recommendations of reports on the basis of certain knowledge and consideration, rather than 'nodding them through', automatically and thoughtlessly.

Again, as chair you should be clear about what's been agreed about any recommendations in reports.

## 4.7 Standard agenda items, 4: any other business

Many agendas will include, after the main discussion items, an item with the words 'Any other business'. This can be a trap for the unwary chair. What it can offer is the opportunity for any member of the meeting to ride a personal hobby-horse, re-open a subject already discussed, or make irrelevant observations. The result can be a lengthy extension to the meeting, just at the time when patience is in short supply and members are eyeing their watches.

There's a place for 'Any other business', but it's a limited place. Under it the chair should only allow time for an issue that meets all of these conditions:

* it should be a subject not considered earlier
* it should be entirely relevant to the work of the group
* it should require attention there and then
* it should be of sufficient importance to deserve attention,

but not so important that it warrants treatment as a substantive item on the agenda

These strict rules apply to the chair, too, in case you're thinking about raising your own issue!

Chair:  Has anyone something to raise under 'Any other business'?
Emil:   Could we have a brief discussion about training needs?
Chair:  Good idea, we've forgotten about them: that's worth a few minutes. Any other matters?
Joanna: I'd like to go back to our decision on the merger. I still don't think we were right to go the way we did ...
Chair:  Hold on, Joanna. We had a very full discussion earlier, and although it wasn't a unanimous decision we agreed that it should stand. I don't think we can re-open the question now.

One way of managing 'Any other business' is to try to identify items members will wish to raise under it at the start of the meeting. The rules of some formal meetings insist that the only items accepted are those notified in advance of the meeting. Remember that in the end it's up to you as chair whether or not to accept a topic for discussion under 'Any other business'.

# 5

# *Conducting the meeting, 2: dynamics*

The core of a well-balanced meeting is not the standard agenda items mentioned in Chapter 4 but the group's treatment of the substantive themes identified on the agenda as the main items for discussion. It's in these extended discussions – usually complex and multi-vocal, sometimes discordant or unfocussed – that the skills and the leadership of the chair are tested most stringently. This chapter suggests how a chair can ensure a positive discussion and overcome some of the main problems that may occur during its course.

## 5.1 Orchestrating discussion

The role of the chair is to make it easier for the group members to work together, to give them the power and time to think and act together. The way to do this is by listening to them, encouraging their participation, and avoiding distractions – while at the same time keeping a constant eye on the task in hand.

Even when the topic has been introduced carefully, its scope has been accurately defined and the members have been thoroughly prepared for an informed debate, the discussion may take unexpected turns. It may become heated and hostile, or the opposite – subdued, circular and muddled. What can the chair do to ensure the best possible chance of a constructive discussion and a positive outcome?

First of all, ask yourself what you would expect to emerge from the discussion. Do you have a strong personal view on the subject, or an ideal outcome? Or do you feel less strong, or even indifferent, towards the issue? Do you want to hear all the arguments before arriving at a private view? The answers to these questions will be crucial to how you guide the conversation. Whether you reveal your preference to the rest of the group is another, separate question. You may decide you don't wish to affect the direction of the discussion, so that all shades of opinion can be heard, or to avoid the appearance of being dictatorial – though you could intervene later on if the tenor of the conversation appears to move in a direction you find unacceptable. On the other hand, when you have a strong sense that your view will command wide or total support you may wish to give the group a strong and unambiguous steer from the beginning (while bearing in mind that you could be wrong!). This has the advantage of avoiding the lengthy rehearsal of hypothetical arguments that will add nothing to the character of the outcome.

Perhaps the most difficult choice you'll face is on the rare occasion when the group's consensus on an issue of real importance to you is directly opposed to your strong belief. Should you yield to the majority view, despite knowing that it would create difficulties for you, or do you attempt to make your view prevail, at the expense of damaging your relations with the group and breaking one of the rules of chairing, 'do not domineer'? There is no simple answer to this question, but two things you could usefully ask yourself are:

- If I let the group have its way, will it become impossible or very difficult to achieve the objectives the group exists to fulfil?
- Will my position become so compromised that I'll find it hard to carry on as chair in future?

If you do dissent from the group's decision, you should consider insisting that your view is formally recorded in the minutes.

Next, think about how to induce a healthy debate. Here a lot will depend on the interplay between two factors: the nature of the group, for example whether the members are confident, articulate and engaged enough to sustain a lively dialogue, and the nature of the subject: could it be too specialised or complex to generate informed opinions?

With luck the introduction to the discussion will have provoked enough thoughts in the minds of some members to enable the conversation to begin. If you suspect, though, that the debate will be slow to catch fire, try posing a single question you're confident will elicit a reaction, and aim it at a specific individual you can normally rely on for a cogent or interesting contribution.

Be conscious of the danger that the conversation will fail to take off, not in the sense that silence will fall, but because the participants are too grounded in patterns of thought that come most readily. An extreme example of this tendency is when someone says, almost as soon as discussion has begun, 'This is always how we've done things,' thereby closing down other paths of exploration. In fact, it doesn't come naturally to most people to take the opposite inclination: to say things like, 'Let's forget about what we did before' or 'Why don't we sit back and think about all the other possibilities?' It's the responsibility of the chair to guard against over-familiar or unadventurous patterns of thought, and to challenge members to think anew.

Once discussion is happily under way you can let the dialogue flow, and direct the conversation with a light touch. That doesn't mean you can afford to sit back and relax, or read the papers for the next item.

It's a good habit to take quick notes on the discussion as it goes on. The secretary, of course, is responsible for the official record of the meeting, but you'll find it helpful to be able to refer back to the main points made, especially when you sum up the discussion at the end.

More important, you'll need to use your listening skills at all times, and be prepared to intervene if necessary. You might need to intervene for several reasons:

- to influence the direction of the discussion: for example, if it threatens to become repetitive or irrelevant, or if time is running out
- to influence the flow of the discussion: in case, for example, conflict between members is in danger of getting out of hand, or discussion is becoming monopolised by just one or two members, or if it has become unproductive
- to influence the understanding of the discussion, so that everyone, including you, is able to grasp what's being said or proposed

## 5.2 Influencing the direction of discussion

Your biggest enemy is usually time. You may have set a time limit for the discussion at the start, but it's unlikely that anyone else in the group will remember that you have. It's all too easy to find that you're rapidly running out of time to complete the discussion satisfactorily, so keep your watch handy and refer to it frequently as the discussion goes on. It does no harm to remind the group's members that time is pressing and that they should keep their contributions concise. Every group has at least one member who likes the sound of their own voice: don't allow them to continue once they've made their essential point.

Once agreement has been reached on one issue, move the debate on as soon as possible to the next, before repetition sets in.

Be alert to occasions when the conversation wanders away into pathways quite irrelevant to the subject in question. Don't hesitate to guide erring members back onto the main road. Occasionally such digressions can have creative results, but you can tolerate them only in more relaxed meetings, like 'away days' or longer facilitated discussions, when time limits are less important (see section 7.7). A related danger is that the discussion, though still relevant to the subject, has started to lose connection with the facts. One way this can happen is when individual members bolster their arguments with evidence drawn exclusively from their personal experience or other anecdotal evidence, unsupported by more broadly based evidence (as gathered, for example, in a paper submitted to the meeting).

Experience of meetings makes it easier to recognise and deal with the different types of members and their behaviours. Here are a few of the more common characters, the kinds of things they say, how they behave, and how you might deal with them:

| The members: what they say and how they behave | The chair: what's the best response? |
|---|---|
| **Mr Snapdragon** 'Just what you'd expect from Darren: that's a *ridiculous* idea!' Quick to criticise ideas, and his fellow members. Rigid in his own views, he rushes into the argument without thought and with few positive ideas. Likes a fight. | Keep cool yourself, and pour oil on his troubled waters. Aim to separate criticism of ideas from personal disparagement. Ask for an apology from him if one is justified. Put him on the spot by inviting him to give his own views. |
| **Ms Primrose** 'Point of order, Chair, point of order, please!' Hot on procedural niceties. Likes to point out errors and inaccuracies. Can't see the wood for the trees. Hasn't got much to offer on the substantial matters. | Deal positively but efficiently with her details (make sure you've mastered the rules and procedures yourself). Put her analytical skills to use in tasks like report writing that require precision and care. |
| **Mr Foxglove** 'I think you'll find, Chair, that some of us aren't happy with that decision. Can we revisit it please – I've had another thought?' Wily and conspiratorial. Out to undermine the group and the authority of the chair. Pushes his own agenda at the expense of the group's larger aims. | Be aware of the hidden agenda and motives behind his words. Flush them out into the open, if it's safe to do so. In any case, don't allow yourself to be distracted: keep the group's eyes on the primary goals. If it comes to a showdown, stage it outside the meeting, away from the other members. |
| **Ms Violet** 'I'm not sure I've anything to add. I'm happy to go along with what's been said.' She says so little, it's hard to know whether she has plenty to contribute but she's too timid to speak up, or whether she's just not interested or engaged. | Get to know her outside the formal meeting. Encourage her to join in when you think she's most likely to. Praise her when she does speak. If she's still uncomfortable in meetings seek other roles in the group that better suit her strengths. |

| Mr Bindweed | |
|---|---|
| 'Bear with me, I've just got three more points to make. I'll be as brief as I can.' Means well, but finds it hard to contain the rapid proliferation of words and ideas. Doesn't mind – or doesn't notice – that he's dominating the room and excluding others. | Stem the torrent of words (courteously), thank him for his views, and invite others to have their say. Even better, ask them to offer their opinions first, and call him into the discussion later. |
| **Mrs Nigella** | |
| 'We tried that idea five years ago, and it didn't work then. Why will it work now?' Instinctively conservative, relentlessly negative, and generally lugubrious. Often an old stager with a long memory. Can have a depressive effect on a cheerful discussion. | Respect her experience but don't let her pile on the misery. Throw her a challenge, asking her for a new and constructive perspective on the matter under discussion. Identify the issue or activity that does engage her enthusiasm, and guide her towards it. |

If, despite your best efforts, your timetable does start to go awry, what should you do? One response is to 'plough on', at the risk of lengthening the meeting and antagonising members, or even losing members who need to leave by a particular time. You may have little choice, but first consider whether there are alternatives. These might include re-ordering the agenda, promoting items of real importance and relegating less essential topics, or even postponing items to the next meeting. Another, more drastic move would be to propose that the members delegate consideration of an important topic for which there's no time in the current meeting to a sub-group or a specific individual, with instructions to refer recommendations back to the main group for a final decision at its next meeting. (This is a useful stratagem in another situation: one of deadlocked or highly conflicted debate.)

There's another, more insidious, danger as you move towards a conclusion to the discussion: that a single solution may emerge too easily, without anyone putting it under real scrutiny. This often happens as a result of 'groupthink'. This is the tendency, especially among people who habitually look at the world in a very similar way, to reinforce, rather than challenge, one another's views, out of anxiety to maintain the harmony of the group and reduce conflict to a minimum. The term 'groupthink' was coined by the American writer Irving Janis, who applied it to the processes that led to disastrous decisions by the US government, such as the Bay of Pigs invasion of Cuba in 1961.[12]

Often the incidence of groupthink has its origin in the initial constitution of the group – one reason for making sure that it contains a variety of viewpoints. But even groups with a heterogeneous composition can be anxious to agree too readily, once they've developed a feeling of solidarity (which the chair may have been responsible for nurturing). You should be aware of what groupthink can lead to. There are several techniques for guarding against it:

- act as devil's advocate to stimulate thinking about alternatives, or turn to a member you can trust to be critical and encourage them to perform the same function
- ask the less dominant members of the group to express their view before turning to more senior or powerful members
- insist that before a solution is agreed the group conducts an 'options appraisal', if this has not already been done: run through the possible choices to make sure that the 'obvious' one really is the right answer
- acquire an outsider's view before a final decision, as a 'reality check' from someone not already attuned to the group's thinking processes
- in general, encourage group members to use their critical faculties when examining complex issues

---

[12] Irving L. Janis, *Groupthink: Psychological Studies of Policy Decisions and Fiascos*, 2nd ed., Boston: Houghton Mifflin, 1983.

| Chair: | So everyone seems to be agreed that the telephone service should close? |
|---|---|
| Members: | [nods all round; some: 'Yes, definitely.'] |
| Chair: | Before we take a decision, maybe we should see the decision from the perspective of people who don't have internet access. Barbara? |
| Barbara: | But none of our own customers fall into that group ... |
| Carlos: | Hmm, I'm not so sure, Barbara, now you mention it. |
| Ophelia: | I came across one the other day who didn't own a computer. Maybe we should spend a bit longer on this discussion. |

A related danger is 'false consensus'. This time it's the chair that's the problem. If the chair asks the question, at the end of the discussion, 'So I assume we're all in agreement?', the answer may appear to be unanimously positive, not because everyone is in agreement, but because they defer to the chair's authority and are reluctant to question it openly. (Mutterings in the corridor afterwards, though, will expose the lack of commitment.) The only way to avoid this phenomenon is for the chair to emphasise honesty in discussion, ask open rather than leading questions, summarise the debate fairly, and avoid giving the impression of omniscience.

A variant of the false consensus is the 'false compromise'. This is where your anxiety as chair to engineer a settlement that pleases every differing standpoint in the group leads to an unclear, contradictory or confused decision. Give and take is a natural and desirable process in treating an issue that divides opinion, but you shouldn't press the principle too far if you're convinced that a poor decision will be the result.

## 5.3 Influencing the flow of discussion
If you've started the meeting well, that is, if you've set everyone

at ease and introduced the agenda item effectively, the conversation should flow smoothly. The word 'conversation' derives from a Latin word meaning 'keep turning over', and that is your role. You can help it revolve quite unobtrusively – making it clear that you're paying close attention to what's said, watching out for members wishing to speak and cueing them in if necessary, nodding encouragement, asking an open question, gently steering discussion forward. You'll have to do very little if your group is working strongly, but if it falters it's your job to lead it forwards.

Four kinds of difficulty can arise with the flow of conversation:

• when it becomes too exclusive
• when it overheats
• when it slows to a standstill
• when discussion is derailed or 'hijacked'

Discussion can easily be captured by the more voluble members at the expense of others who are quieter or even completely silent. It's common for a chair, caught up in the intellectual cut and thrust of an argument, not to notice that there are members who, though they may have valuable views to express, feel discouraged or even intimidated by the force of personality or the strength of argument shown by the dominant speakers. You're in a position to correct the imbalance, and you should remind yourself throughout the meeting of the danger.

A general appeal for views from others may not be enough. You may need to create a gap in the flow of conversation by suggesting, politely, that talkative members have had enough opportunity to speak, and then turn to the silent members and ask them, individually if necessary, to offer an opinion. Sometimes people are taken aback if the chair singles them out by name, but it is a legitimate tactic and has the additional benefit of keeping people alert if they're less than fully engaged in the discussion.

If you suspect from the beginning that there's likely to be an imbalance of contributors, you could go round the table at a suitable point, perhaps before you reach complex or difficult subjects, and ask the members to give their views in turn. This should signal to more reticent members that their views are valued, and help to give them confidence.

At other times the flow of the discussion can become turbulent and heated. For a chair conflict between participants is acceptable, and can be creative, with two qualifications: that it doesn't get out of control, and that it isn't personal. When those conditions aren't met, you need to intervene, without becoming involved yourself in the argument or losing your own temper. One method of cooling the emotional temperature is to invoke two of the traditional customs of formal meetings, that members should speak one at a time, without interrupting others, and that they should address their remarks to the chair, not one another. If a member criticises others or their views in an entirely negative way, try asking them to set out their own views: this can deflate anger and restore a constructive tone. If debate has developed an adversarial and polarised nature, try to restore it to what it should be: a joint exploration of a subject. In his book *The Devil's Dictionary* (1911), the American satirist Ambrose Bierce naughtily defined 'discussion' as 'a method of confirming others in their errors'. But such rigidity of position is something to be avoided. It shuts down other arguments, discourages people from expressing more nuanced positions, and can lead to 'trench warfare' extending into the future. Think about why members have shown aggression. It may stem from anxiety or fear or stress, or a history of personal animosity. Understanding the causes should suggest ways of countering or disarming the conflict.

If all else fails, you could consider calling a break in the meeting, to allow tempers to cool and compromises to emerge. This is a common Speaker's tactic in the House of Commons, a group so rowdy and ill-behaved that few chairs of any sense would choose to preside over it.

Very occasionally disaffected members turn on the chair rather than against other members, rather as a frustrated football manager will round on an innocent referee. This usually takes the form of sniping rather than a frontal assault. Snipers will often start with the words, 'With great respect, Chair ...' and go on to pick a fight on a matter of procedure. They might claim, for example, that the chair has failed to allow an amendment to a motion to be put to a vote, or has curtailed a speech in opposition to the majority opinion. Any chair familiar with the rules of debate will seldom be bothered by this kind of attack (see section 7.1).

| | |
|---|---|
| Benedict: | You can't allow that, Chair – that's absurd. Ruth's already spoken, she can't have another bite at the cherry. This discussion's becoming very one-sided, and you keep favouring certain speakers. |
| Chair: | Ben, I do my best to treat everyone in the same way. Ruth has a perfect right to speak. When she spoke earlier it was in favour of the motion, but now we're discussing Ted's amendment to the motion. There's nothing in our rules to prevent her. Ruth, please continue ... |

You might face not antagonism and excitement, but their opposite. The discussion begins to flag as the healthy winds of argument fade away and a sultry, wearying torpor descends on the group. Discussion falters, no one seems able to offer a new perspective or a way forward, views already expressed are repeated. This is a time when the chair should step in decisively. There are several possibilities:

- 're-boot' the discussion by restating the arguments used so far and reminding members of what they might have forgotten
- act as 'devil's advocate' by challenging an assumption made in the discussion

- throw in an entirely new idea to stimulate fresh thinking
- admit that a conclusion is unlikely now and postpone a decision, but arrange a mechanism outside the meeting, for example a small group, to bring a conclusion closer

You need to be alert to another possibility: not excessive conflict or stagnation in the discussion, but occasions when members with their own agendas try to divert the conversation into their personal areas. Their motives may vary: trying to build their own power bases or empires, riding personal hobby-horses, flying private 'kites' to gauge the reaction of others, scoring points against other members, currying favour with or perhaps challenging the chair, or an anxiety to demonstrate intellectual leadership or social pre-eminence within the group. You should deal with this kind of intervention politely but with firmness, and recall the meeting to the business in hand. It's unlikely that doing so will lose you any credit with other members.

Another kind of misbehaviour in a meeting is when two or more members start to hold a private conversation, in parallel with or in competition with the general discussion. This can happen for innocent or less innocent reasons, but either way you should put a swift end to it.

## 5.4 Influencing the understanding of a discussion

Even if you feel you've a good grasp of the discussion, don't assume everyone does. During its course, and certainly at its conclusion, you should try to summarise by paraphrasing the main points and reflect back your understanding to the members. This will give them the chance to correct or challenge you, and avoid progressing on the basis of false or unshared assumptions.

What if it turns out that there's general confusion or a lack of understanding? Rather than continue the discussion you could change gear and suggest different approaches, all of which could help the members clarify and advance their thinking:

- go back to first principles and ask what outcomes the group should be seeking to achieve
- divide the group into small sub-groups and ask them to find answers to questions that tackle parts of the problem; when combining the results, use visual aids like adhesive notes, whiteboards or flipcharts
- again in small groups, use techniques borrowed from other, more exploratory kinds of group in order to release new lines of creativity; for example:
  - brainstorming, with its rapid production of ideas and ban on initial criticism of them
  - techniques of charting ideas and the connections linking them, like Tony Buzan's 'mind maps'[13] and Peter Checkland's 'rich pictures'[14]
  - Edward de Bono's 'Six Thinking Hats'[15], which encourages people to see the same problem from multiple perspectives in parallel.
    (These exercises may require the services of a separate facilitator: see section 7.7.)
- commission a report or presentation from someone who's not a member of the group, to introduce new information and a different perspective

---

[13] Tony Buzan, with Chris Griffiths and James Harrison, *Modern Mind Mapping for Smarter Thinking*, Cardiff: Proactive Press, 2012. http://thinkbuzan.com/
[14] Peter Checkland and John Poulter, *Learning for Action: A Short Definitive Account of Soft Systems Methodology and Its Use for Practitioners, Teachers and Students*, Chichester: Wiley, 2006. http://en.wikipedia.org/wiki/Rich_picture
[15] Edward de Bono, *Six Thinking Hats*, rev. ed., London: Penguin, 2000. http://www.debonogroup.com/six_thinking_hats.php

Chair:     So that's the motion. Is everyone sure what we're
           going to vote on? Do say if you're uncertain about any
           part of it.
Davina:    I must admit, I'm not completely clear about how the
           new insurance system's going to work.
Ken:       I thought I was, but now I'm not so sure.
Chair:     Fine. Becca, you're our expert on insurance. Could you
           describe the process in simple terms, maybe with the
           help of a diagram on the whiteboard?

## 5.5 Reaching decisions

If the quality of the discussion is important, its conclusion is critical. This is where the chair has three crucial tasks to perform:

- summarise the arguments
- ensure the group arrives at a clear decision
- agree what will happen next as a result of taking the decision

How far you need to *sum up the arguments* will depend on the importance of the topic and the obviousness of the reasons for a decision. If the subject is relatively simple, the decision easy to reach and the reasons for it clear, there's little point in rehearsing the arguments in depth. On the other hand, if the discussion has been complex or contested, and especially if you see a possible need in future to refer back to the reasons behind a decision, it's wise to summarise the main arguments, including those of the minority view.

The next stage is to *get the group to reach a clear decision*. Often a consensus will emerge naturally. The chair's role is confined to articulating the conclusion with clarity. But remember to check that everyone present is content with the decision as you've expressed it. Don't assume that, just because no one has expressed dissent so far, everyone is convinced. Some members may have suppressed their doubts, or have had second thoughts or a late change of mind. If you're not entirely certain that everyone is wholly supportive, go round the table and ask each member individually for their view.

At other times conflicting views can develop, without an obvious way of either reconciling them or deciding between them becoming clear. This can be frustrating for everyone, and the members will turn to you to suggest or engineer a way forward. These are some of the stratagems you might consider:

- get the group to revisit the evidential basis of each viewpoint: this may reveal previously unsuspected weaknesses in arguments
- bring new evidence or new views to bear, perhaps from outside the group, after calling an adjournment in the discussion
- review again the possible options and weigh up their strengths and weaknesses
- agree not to force the issue to a decision, if this is possible ...
- ... or if it's not possible, put the matter to a vote, but only after ensuring that the losing party will accept the final conclusion in good part

As a last resort the chair could impose a solution. In relatively unimportant matters this may be acceptable, but a diktat from the chair with regard to a complex matter or one of principle is risky and could threaten your authority.

Some chairs, in some circumstances, use their authority to force decisions by stifling discussion and suppressing dissent. John Mackintosh, the historian of the British Cabinet,[16] recalls that Prime Minister Clement Attlee's aim in Cabinet meetings was to avoid objections being raised, often through his use of the negative question:

---

[16] John Mackintosh, *The British Cabinet*, 3rd edition, London: Stevens, 1977, p.502.

| Attlee: | Does any member of the Cabinet oppose this? |
| A member: | An interesting case occurred in 1929 which was very similar to this, and I remember that we ... |
| Attlee: | Do you oppose this? |
| The member: | Er ... No. |
| Attlee: | Very good – that is settled. |

But few of us enjoy Attlee's kind of dominance, or would wish to copy his methods.

However you get there, what's important is that you ensure that a clear decision has been reached. Restate what you believe has been agreed and decided. Sometimes it's tempting to skip this stage and assume that everyone will know exactly what they've just decided, but even in the simplest cases this assumption may be wrong. Some members may have misunderstood, or fallen into a reverie. It's all too easy to *feel* an unambiguous decision has been reached, only to find that it's less clear than you thought when you try to establish it in black and white. The minute-writer shouldn't have to bear the burden of this discovery after the fact. In a formal meeting, where a motion has been debated, you should read out the text word for word, since it's likely that every phrase has been scrutinised during the discussion.

If it's proved impossible to gain unanimity and there are one or more members who are not content, they may wish their disagreement to be recorded in the minutes of the meeting. In a formal meeting the numbers, and sometimes names, of those in favour or against a motion, and those abstaining, are recorded.

For each group member there's an ascending ladder of agreement to any important decision:

conviction

assent

consent

*Consent* is the least committed form of agreement. It could be expressed simply as silence – a lack of dissent – or as a purely formal action, like a vote in favour. *Assent* implies a more positively expressed agreement, for example a statement in favour of a motion. *Conviction* implies that members are so confident about the decision that they treat it as their own. If the matter under discussion is one that's of critical importance to your group, you should as chair do all you can to ensure that your members are indeed convinced that the right decision has been taken. It may not be obvious immediately that a member is truly committed, but might well be clear indirectly, for example through a willingness to promote the decision voluntarily outside the group.

Once the group has taken a decision the next question is: what happens next? You should *make sure that the members agree how the decision will be put into practice*. There's little point in coming to a decision if no one's sure what's going to happen next. So, as chair you should establish reasonable targets for:

- *how* the decision will be acted upon
- *who* will be responsible for carrying out the actions
- *by when* they will be carried out

Each of these should be written into the minutes alongside the record of the decision, and in any list of 'action points', so that the group can easily check on progress at the next meeting. This process of identifying practical steps to implement a decision acts as a useful check on how practical the decision really is. You might realise that implementation is going to be very difficult and conclude – unwelcome though this realisation may be – that you'll need to revisit the decision itself.

'Who?' is a particularly important question. Even if some organisation or individual outside the group is going to be in charge of implementation, normally someone inside the group itself will have to start the ball rolling. This might be the chair or it could be any other member, depending on their relevance to the topic. Delegating responsibility for actions to other members isn't just natural and appropriate. It can also be a useful way of sharing the burden of work, promoting the personal development of individuals, and building trust and a sense of ownership within the group.

| | |
|---|---|
| Chair: | Thank you for that decision. It's one of the most important we've taken this year, would that be true to say? |
| Eveline: | Yes, I agree. I think we've taken a big step forward. |
| Steve: | It's good that all our hard work's paid off. |
| Chair: | We need a plan to put the decision into action. Eveline, would you be happy to convene a small group to produce one? With help from Steve? |
| Eveline and Steve: | Yes, of course. |
| Chair: | And could we include you too, Basil? |
| Basil: | Well, you know I argued against, but yes, I'd be happy to help. |

If the decision is far-reaching it might carry secondary implications, which you should also think about, now or after the meeting:

- *Who will be affected* by the decision?
- *Who needs to know* about the decision, and how?
- *What other decisions* will follow from this one?

Ask yourself what other organisations or people will make of your decisions, now and in the future. Are there going to be legal, financial or publicity repercussions? The chair of a child protection case conference, for example, must take great care that the committee's decisions are fully and accurately documented, as the case could become the subject of a later enquiry, which would scrutinise the group's work in detail.

You're now ready to move on to the next item, but, before you do, try to make sure that you leave this discussion on a positive note – even, or especially, if it's been contentious.

## 5.6 Concluding the meeting

Once you've exhausted the agenda the meeting should be complete. With luck you'll have finished by the time set for the end of the meeting, or even before. No one has ever been heard to voice the criticism, 'I'm a bit disappointed, Chair, that the meeting has finished early'.

You should wind up quickly, but not before you:

- remind members of the date, time and place of the next meeting
- thank everyone for coming and contributing (with special thanks to any guests, to those who submitted papers or made presentations, and to the secretary)
- remind the group of the importance of their work and what's been achieved so far (you need people to relish, not fear, the prospect of the next meeting!)

You could also ask the members, especially members of a new group, if they think the way the meeting functions could be improved in future. Some chairs ask them to score the effectiveness of the meeting formally, for instance, on a scale of one to five. This is a practice of doubtful value, even if you can rely on members to give an honest appraisal. It can be unclear whether a low score reflects badly on the group or on you, and it's equally unclear, at least without prolonged discussion at a time when most people are keen to leave, how to improve matters. There are other and better ways of evaluating how well the group and the chair are performing (see section 6.7).

Unless this is the very final meeting of your group, its end doesn't mean that you can sit back and relax. As well as dealing with the outcomes of this meeting and preparing for the next, you should be giving some thought to how to sustain and nurture the group in the meantime.

## 5.7 Following up the meeting

The first thing to do is to make sure that you have a true and accurate record of the meeting. The secretary should write the draft minutes as soon as possible afterwards, before memory fades or notes become indecipherable, and show them to you (you could agree a deadline). Don't hesitate to query anything that doesn't seem accurate or to suggest there might be information missing. Make sure that the minutes include the actions agreed in the meeting, and the names of those responsible for carrying them out (and by when).

Some secretaries don't send minutes out to members until they distribute the agenda and papers of the next meeting. But this could be weeks after the original meeting. It's much better to send the minutes promptly, as soon as you've approved them as chair. All members, including those who were absent, will then have an account of the meeting and its decisions, and will be able to check who's responsible for the actions agreed. The secretary may seek any corrections that members notice straight away, though they will only be confirmed formally when approved at the next meeting.

Some organisations make the minutes of their meetings available to the public after their confirmation. If so, you may need to 'redact' or edit out any minutes that contain confidential or personal information that should not be published.

Your second task is to follow up the actions agreed and the implications of decisions taken at the meeting. It's likely that some of the actions are for you to fulfil. Others were left to other group members. Experience will tell you how great a degree of confidence you can place in them to complete their commissions. Some chairs make a practice of contacting members who have actions to carry out a day or two after the meeting, to thank them for their work and remind them of what they've undertaken to do before the next meeting. In any case it's usually worth checking up on those actions that are critical to the progress of the group's aims before planning the next meeting.

Thirdly, if your group reports to another body or individual you may need to report the outcomes of the meeting, either in written form, through the minutes or your own summary, or in person through attending a meeting of the parent body or talking to the individual to whom your group is answerable. In addition, consider whether other people would benefit from knowing what's been agreed in the meeting. The committee of a voluntary group may feel, for example, that all the members of the group should be informed about its decisions as soon as possible through a newsletter, email circular or Facebook posting.

And then the cycle begins all over again, with preparations for the next meeting. This is when all the 'follow up' actions will be reviewed, many of them in the course of going through 'Matters arising' from the minutes.

# 6

## *Chairs, boards and chief executives*

In many groups the chair is the single leader. But in some circumstances the locus of power and responsibility is not so concentrated. This is especially true when the chair presides over a formal body overseeing the work of an established organisation that has its own chief executive and paid staff. Two examples of this situation are the board of a stand-alone public body or charity and the board of a commercial company.

Boards of this kind have real power and very often legal and financial duties, so chairing them is a serious business, not to be taken on lightly. It's a rather different task from, say, chairing an advisory board, which, though it may have an important, even constitutional role in an organisation, lacks the authority or responsibilities of a governing board.

## 6.1 Chairing the board of a public body

The public body or charity may receive its funding from central or local government or other public sources, but will have its own independent existence, derived from a statute, Royal Charter or other document, its own written constitution, and its own staff. It's likely to be led by a chief executive, or chief executive Officer (CEO), or someone with a different title but the same functions: directing the strategy, operations and resources of the body, and taking responsibility for its performance. In the case of a larger body the chief executive will usually have a senior team of managers, each of them specialising in a particular area of activity, who together assist with developing policy and with the overall operation of the body.

Sitting above this executive structure will be the board. In a charity its members, who perhaps number around fifteen, are likely to be the trustees of the charity, responsible in law for the good regulation of the charity's purposes and activity. The board's functions are usually to decide on corporate issues, strategic direction and major issues of policy, oversee the finances, and hold the chief executive to account.

Not surprisingly the chair of the board has much more to do than the chair of a less formal or complex group. It isn't simply a question of turning up to preside over meetings four or five times a year. The main differences are these:

- the body is an established and permanent one, with persistent functions or services to perform; its tasks will not come to a final conclusion
- there's a separate person, the chief executive, responsible for executing the body's strategy and policies, and the board's decisions
- the chair and the other board members may be legally and financially accountable for the activities of the body
- the chair (and occasionally the other board members) may sometimes be paid for their services
- how the chair, the board and the body operate will be specified by formal rules
- the board is likely to have subordinate committees reporting to it on particular subjects
- meetings, the operation of which will also be determined formally, are important, but there are other ways in which the chair will interact with the body, and especially with the chief executive

Formality affects the role of the Chair directly. It's a post whose appointment is often subject to advertisement and competitive recruitment, under the terms of what are still called 'Nolan' rules, after Lord Nolan who chaired the UK Committee on Standards in Public Life set up in 1994. The aim of the rules is to ensure fairness and transparency in appointment to public bodies, in order to remove suspicion that appointments are made on any basis other than the merit of the successful candidate. The appointment process is controlled by a formal panel that will include one or more independent members. This doesn't mean that potential chairs can't be approached to see whether they would be willing to consider applying – there might be a preference for someone who's already familiar with the body, or has even been a board member – or that chief executives might not have ideas about possible candidates (though they should not take an active part in the recruitment process).

Lord Nolan's committee also drew up what are known as the Seven Principles of Public Life, which should regulate the behaviour of those in public positions. The Principles are: selflessness, integrity, objectivity, accountability, openness, honesty and leadership (the last in the restricted sense of taking the lead in promoting the other principles). They are intended to apply to all those working in or for public bodies, including non-departmental public bodies (in other words those semi-independent public bodies that are likely to have boards and chairs).

Another consequence of increased formality is that the roles and functions of the chair, and the board as a whole, are likely to be set out on paper in the charter or other document governing the body. Among the matters covered in this way may be:

- the method of appointment of the chair and other officers
- their periods of office, and any provision for re-appointment
- whether the chair is paid (for example, remuneration and expenses)
- the role of chairing meetings of the board
- the nature, composition and chairing of any board committees
- the number and nature of board meetings
- the powers of the board members

These provisions may well be supplemented by other, subordinate written rules, for example about the relationship between the board and the chief executive, rules laid down by funding bodies about the board's approval of plans, and 'standing orders' for the conduct of meetings.

All this means that as chair of a board you need to master the formal duties of your situation carefully before starting work. As well as reading the relevant documents, you may find that the body organises an induction session for new board members to introduce you to your legal and organisational responsibilities and to the work of the body itself. If one isn't offered, you could ask for an informal session, and in any case you'll certainly need several conversations with the chief executive and the senior team to learn about their continuing work and current projects.

It's also worth speaking informally with each of your fellow board members. This will alert you to matters that concern them and give you an overall feel for the health of the organisation. It will give them a chance to get to know you outside the context of a meeting. The members will bring different skills and kinds of expertise to the board. They may have been appointed on the basis of a call for specific areas of competence in the advertisement for their posts. From talking to them informally you'll learn something about the strength of their contribution.

It's possible that you're not the only officer on the board. There may be a vice-chair, or other specific posts, such as treasurer, and some members may be chairs of Board committees, like the audit committee. You should find talks with the holders of these posts especially helpful. Make sure you know what their powers and duties are, and how they relate to your own.

Check, too, whether all the board members are truly independent or whether some of them represent the interests of outside organisations, like funders or other stakeholders. (Charity trustees are expected to 'forget' who appointed them and to act only in the interests of the charity.) This distinction can carry important implications, for accountability, confidentiality and conflicts of interest. Even if they're all independent, some board members may be there because they're regarded as good fundraisers rather than as 'all-rounders': the chair should be aware of the balance between the different pressures on members.

Finally, try to judge how much time you'll need to spend on board work – not just on meetings, but on reading, writing and communicating with other people. An advertisement for the post of chair will often give an estimate of how many days a month will be needed. This can turn out be an underestimate, especially if you face major tasks or crises during your period.

## 6.2 Chairing the board of a company

It's common for a commercial organisation, and essential for a public company, to have a board of directors, presided over by a paid chair, which is responsible for the overall governance of the organisation. (A charity may also be incorporated as a limited company, or may own a company.) In the words of the Financial Reporting Council, the role of the board is to 'provide entrepreneurial leadership of the company within a framework of prudent and effective controls which enables risk to be assessed and managed'.[17]

There are three possible types of board chair:

- the chair is an executive chair, sitting above the chief executive in the company's hierarchy and wielding direct power and operational influence. This arrangement is common in the United States, but significantly less so in the UK.
- the role of chair is combined with that of the chief executive or managing director, as in 'chair and chief executive'. This arrangement is found in smaller companies and some larger ones.
- the chair is non-executive, and doesn't get involved in the day-to-day operation of the company. This is common in larger and public companies.

---

[17] Financial Reporting Council, *Guidance on Board Effectiveness*, London: FRC, 2011, p.2
https://www.frc.org.uk/getattachment/c9ce2814-2806-4bca-a179-e390ecbed841/Guidance-on-Board-Effectiveness.aspx

The UK Corporate Governance Code (2012), echoing many earlier authorities, rejects the second model, stating that 'there should be a clear division of responsibilities at the head of the company between the running of the board and the executive responsibility for the running of the company's business. No one individual should have unfettered powers of decision [...] The roles of chairman and chief executive should not be exercised by the same individual'.[18] The tide was already running against the merging of the two roles: shareholders of Marks & Spencer rebelled after Stuart Rose became chair as well as chief executive of the company in 2008. Most companies of any size now split the two posts. This section is therefore concerned only with the non-executive chair.

A company's board of directors is likely to consist of two categories of members:

- executive directors: the Chief Executive and other owners or employees of the company
- non-executive directors: external members, not part of the management of the company, who are recruited for their specialist expertise and network connections

A distinction is commonly made between non-executives who own shares in the company and those termed 'independent non-executive directors', who don't. One of the latter is usually designated as a 'senior independent director'. This person acts as a sounding board for the chair, and also takes the lead role in evaluating the chair's performance and in overseeing the recruitment process for the next chair. They come into their own at times of difficulty, for example when the relationship between

---

[18] Financial Reporting Council, *The UK Corporate Governance Code*, London: Financial Reporting Council, 2012, p.9.
https://www.frc.org.uk/Our-Work/Publications/Corporate-Governance/UK-Corporate-Governance-Code-September-2012.pdf

the chair and the chief executive becomes strained (or too close), or when shareholders are anxious about the strategic or governance direction a public company is taking. Indeed, the senior independent director can act as a general conduit for the shareholders to share their views with the board.

Except for small companies, at least half of the members should be non-executives. The board is responsible for appointing the chair from among the non-executive directors or from outside (but not usually from the executive members). It will normally have a number of committees, for example, for audit, nominations (of new board members) and remuneration.

Company boards, while they usually try to ensure a good mix of skills and knowledge of relevance to the business, have traditionally failed to reflect adequately in the composition of their membership the diversity of the society they operate in, including their employees and customers. A government report in 2011, for example, estimated that it would take over seventy years, at the current rate of change, to achieve gender equality in UK boardrooms (12.5% was the proportion of women in 2010). Some modest improvement has occurred since, mainly among non-executive directors, but an incoming chair could usefully review the gender and ethnic balance of the existing board, and its prevailing culture and ethos.

The main functions of the non-executive chair, who is likely to be part-time, are quite similar to those of the chair of a public body:

- chair meetings of the board, organising its business and ensuring members are given the information they need
- set or confirm the company's strategic direction, values and standards, and assess risks and the adequacy of financial controls
- review and assess the performance of the board and the chief executive
- ensure good communication with the company's shareholders

From the beginning the chair needs to be aware of which issues are proper to this particular board, as opposed to those where the chief executive and the management team have authority. Usually these will concern governance, overall strategy, performance, accountability, compliance and control of risk, and they should be detailed in the company's Articles of Association or similar document.

*Before a meeting* you should plan the agenda carefully. Make sure that the papers to be sent out are relevant and comprehensible. In the course of your preparation you can rely on the services of the company secretary to help you. The company secretary has legal responsibilities under the Companies Act and should be familiar with the formal duties of the board.

In *meetings* the chair needs to bear in mind in particular the presence of the non-executives and their distinctive role. They offer the chance of an external, independent check on what the executive members of the board are proposing: an element of constructive challenge, which can be especially useful when a consensus has developed unopposed. They can bring different skills and particularly experience to the discussion.

For companies the *annual meeting* is an important date in the calendar. This is when shareholders can hear directly from the board and question its members, when the media can report on its performance, and when news of the company can reach the attention of the public. For these reasons thorough preparation for the meeting, and of the annual report presented at it, is essential. In the meeting it's normal for the chair to speak about the leadership and effectiveness of the board, even if the chief executive takes the lead on presenting information on the performance of the company.

Your tasks as chair *outside meetings* of the board will probably include:

- ensuring that induction and continuous training are available to board members so that they have a good appreciation of their duties and are familiar with the work of the company, and ensuring that development opportunities are open to promising potential new members of the board

- keeping the composition of the Board under constant review so that it contains the right balance of skills, knowledge and independence, and arranging for the recruitment of new members (often organised through a nomination committee)
- representing the company in the media and in external communications
- upholding the values and the principles the company espouses, for example on environmental matters or the personal behaviour of executives
- supporting and giving advice to the chief executive (see section 6.3)

## 6.3 Working with a chief executive

As a chair of a public body or a company, the most important relationship you'll have is with the chief executive. If the relationship is a good one it will provide a solid basis for the effective governance of the organisation. If it's a poor one, problems are likely to arise. If it's a bad one, the very future of the body can be put in danger. In extreme cases it's been known for both the chair and the chief executive to resign or be removed from office.

Even if the organisation has a statement defining the nature of the relationship it's unlikely that it's very detailed. The reason for this is that beyond one basic principle the success or the failure of the relationship depends on human factors rather than written rules.

The basic principle is that there should be a clear division of responsibilities between the chair and the chief executive. The chair is in charge of the governance of the organisation (its structure of accountability) and its overall direction (its basic strategy). The chief executive takes care of the body's operation (detailed policies and day-to-day running) and its resources (money and staff). The chief executive will certainly have a role in contributing to governance and strategy, but will not have the final say, and must accept what the board decides. Likewise, the chair should take an informed interest in how the organisation works, and be prepared to challenge, but should not interfere in its operation or try to be a 'shadow manager'. The only exception to the 'non-interference' principle is if the chief executive is clearly failing and as chair you need to intervene to prevent the organisation from harm or collapse.

This 'defining of frontiers' is a complex process and hard to codify in a set of rules. So a great deal depends on the human interaction between chair and chief executive. As chair you may have 'inherited' a chief executive, or you may have been responsible for their recruitment, but your first job is to get to know them – well. The relationship that develops doesn't have to be extra-friendly. Indeed, a certain distance is desirable, considering that the chief executive will be answerable to the board through the chair for personal and organisational performance. But it should rest on three essential values: respect, trust and openness. As chair you should:

- have confidence in the chief executive's ability to run the organisation well, and use its financial and human resources effectively
- ask for, and offer, information and advice without hesitation or embarrassment
- not be afraid to offer a challenge as a 'critical friend', or, on the other hand, to ask how you could support the chief executive better

and in turn the chief executive should:

- acknowledge the chair's distinctive role and expertise in co-ordinating the board
- ask for, and offer, information and advice without hesitation or embarrassment

- not conceal major problems or crises, but be willing to discuss them openly; there should be a practice of 'no surprises', so that neither is caught unawares by the actions of the other

A good chair can offer a chief executive many things: support through difficult changes that need to happen, a different perspective on a problem, even a shoulder to cry on when the going is tough. The situation of the chief executive can be a very lonely one and when times are difficult it can help to be able to turn for confidential advice to a chair. The 'frontier' between governance and management is a shifting and permeable one. Sometimes the chief executive will want the chair's advice on an operational matter, for example the behaviour of a particular member of staff, and it would be foolish for the chair to respond, 'But that's your affair, not mine: I won't become involved.' Sometimes an operational matter becomes of concern to the board because it happens to be very sensitive and possibly public in its repercussions. A chair may also be the final stage in an appeal procedure in grievance or disciplinary cases (see section 7.6).

A chair's advice is often best offered obliquely, through listening well and responding to questions, rather than by proffering your wisdom directly. While bringing your experience of other organisations will be a strength, it isn't helpful for a chief executive to hear you say repeatedly, 'When I was in your shoes this is what I used to do ...' Advice can flow in the other direction: the chair might value the chief executive's opinion on how to manage a controversial discussion in a board meeting.

Inevitably the chair and the chief executive will not agree on everything – it would be unhealthy if they did – but as long as there is agreement on the core values and central strategy of the organisation, as well as the right personal 'chemistry' built on respect, trust and openness, the relationship will remain close and strong.

What if these foundations of a strong relationship are lacking? Here are some of the symptoms of a failing relationship:

- communication between the chair and chief executive becomes sparse, and relations cool
- the chief executive hides crucial information from the Chair
- the chief executive is slow to carry out board decisions, or fails to do so
- major problems, external and internal, suddenly appear without warning
- other members of the executive team seek individual access to the chair
- the chair bypasses or contradicts the chief executive by dealing with other officers

The chair has no choice in this situation but to address the problems. Your central task is to try to stabilise relations with the chief executive. Other board members may have crucial roles to play, and it's essential that you have the support of the board for any radical action you plan to take. A particularly difficult situation for the chair is when the chief executive seems to be losing the support of some of the organisation's staff, especially the senior team. It may be that that this is a natural risk of implementing an agreed programme of reform and modernisation. In this case you need to support the chief executive in winning over or overcoming opposition to change. Or it may be that the chief executive has adopted policies without the approval of the board, causing unnecessary conflict. If this happens the chair's role is to help the chief executive reconnect with the board's wishes and repair relationships with other people. It's always best to avoid a showdown with your chief executive, unless you have no other alternative. A head-to-head clash will usually embitter relationships on the board and among the staff, may attract bad publicity, and will certainly distract attention and energies from the proper business of your organisation.

The opposite situation can also develop: where the relationship between the chair and the chief executive becomes too close. 'Groupthink' is always a danger if it reduces scrutiny and excludes alternatives. One of the striking features about the way in which some UK banks almost destroyed themselves in 2008–09 was that, when chief executives pursued disastrous policies of risky lending and over-ambitious acquisition, their chairs, often themselves innocent of the complexities of contemporary banking, failed to restrain them and instead joined in the frenetic madness. Friendship, deference, shared values or the other things that draw people together should never be allowed to extinguish altogether the professional distance that should divide a chair from a chief executive.

Perhaps the most fateful decision a chair may be part of is the recruitment of a new chief executive. You need to approach the entire process with the utmost care and seriousness. A poor decision could spell disaster for your organisation, or at least a tough time for your own successor. Among the critical questions you should ask are:

- Who will be responsible for the recruitment? (A panel of the board?)
- What are the qualities you're seeking in candidates?
- What methods will you use to secure the strongest candidates, and to select the best one among them?

All of these roles may suggest that as chair you're in a rather isolated position at the apex of the organisation. But this shouldn't leave you feeling desolate. You can share your anxieties with your chief executive, with trusted board members, and with external mentors, such as fellow chairs. Being able to discuss things confidentially is an important part of personal resilience.

## 6.4 The functions of the board
The other central relationship is between the chair and the board.

What are the functions of the board? Of course boards – of public bodies or charities or companies – vary in how they are established, but in general they tend to:

- supervise the governance of the organisation
- set its overall strategy
- monitor its performance
- oversee finances
- assess risks
- support its chief executive and staff, and help them excel
- represent the organisation and protect its good name

The board is responsible for guarding the foundations of the organisation's existence and status: its constitution and rules, its organisational structure and how the board itself and its subordinate bodies operate – in short, its *governance*. So it will need to take time to: make sure its constitution is relevant and, if it isn't, to make changes to it; keep its committees under review so that they fulfil their intended purpose; and recruit new members to the board and its committees who will bring the right skills and values to the organisation.

The overall direction of an organisation, its *strategy*, is of critical importance to any board. Forming a strategy is often a process shared between the board and the organisation's staff, and especially the chief executive. The latter should possess the expert knowledge and vision to research and prepare a draft strategy, while board members can bring fresh external perspectives and a sense of challenge. But however the strategy is created, it's the board that has to approve it, and then take ownership of it as the guide to the organisation's development in the period to come.

The chief executive is normally accountable to the board for the progress of the strategy, and indeed for the overall operation and services of the organisation. So *monitoring performance* is a crucial concern for the board. It needs to have effective methods of gauging how well things are going, and members who are

110

prepared to question why targets aren't being met. A particularly important area for constant review is the *financial health* of the body. A board will often delegate detailed financial scrutiny to an audit committee, though it shouldn't and can't divest itself of final responsibility.

The board is ultimately accountable for the success and financial health of the organisation, and so it must keep a close eye on the many kinds of *risk* that could cause injury or even fatal damage. These include: risks to the organisation's reputation; its business continuity; its compliance with law and regulation; and its financial health. Assessing risk is usually by means of a regularly reviewed 'risk register'. The board can delegate the control of operational risks to managers, but it should pay particular attention to the risks inherent in the chief executive's financial proposals and its legal obligations. It needs to feel confident that the level of risk being taken is acceptable. The chair must ensure that these processes are in place.

If monitoring and risk analysis can seem a critical and even negative activity, board members, as a result of coming from outside the organisation, have a more positive function: to *offer support* to the chief executive and the staff. It's true that many people, especially in a public body, feel a strong loyalty to the body they work for, and always wish to do their best, but it makes a great difference for them to know that the people to whom they're ultimately responsible appreciate their dedication and their achievements. But board members can do even more than this. For example, they may be able to remove barriers staff feel are hindering their work, or they might encourage staff to do even better, to find smarter ways of working, or start working in new directions. Ideally the kind of trust that exists between chair and chief executive should also exist between board members and the senior staff of the organisation.

No organisation exists in a vacuum. It interacts with a host of individuals and other bodies – funders, competitors, service users, suppliers, governments and the general public. Its reputation therefore matters. The chair and all board members have their part to play in *representing* their organisation in this external world. In effect they act as ambassadors on its behalf: celebrating its achievements, defending its good name and spreading the word about its excellence.

All these functions are of concern to the board as a whole and its individual members, but the chair, as their leader and chief spokesperson, is the one who carries the responsibility for making sure their roles are fulfilled.

### 6.5 Meetings of the board

Planning and conducting board meetings follow the same general principles described in Chapters 3-5. Planning will usually be quite formalised. For example, meetings of the board and its committees are timetabled at least a year in advance. The detailed arrangements are in the hands of the secretary or clerk, both drawn from the staff of the organisation, and in general the staff supply the other individuals, such as minute-takers and authors of papers, who are necessary for the smooth running of meetings.

Preparing the agenda is important. There are certain to be some standard items, like matters concerning the constitution and the board itself, reports on performance and finance, and reports from the board's committees. You should also find time to discuss strategic issues, such as the planning or progress of large-scale projects. If time allows it's good for the board sometimes to hear presentations from staff about their current work or projects. This helps members understand what's happening at grassroots level, and gives an opportunity for them to show their appreciation to the presenter and by extension to the presenter's colleagues. In meetings that are open to the public, or at least to some external people, there might be a case for dividing the agenda into two: the larger part being 'open' but with discussion of sensitive items, for example those dealing with staffing issues, confined to board members only in a 'closed' session. As with any agenda you should note against each item what members are expected to do (note, discuss or decide), but

– especially when the agenda's very full – you might want to filter into a separate section at the end subjects and papers that are for information or note (unless a member objects).

The more formal the group the more paper it's likely to attract. Some boards of institutions such as universities that are addicted to committees will fling mountains of paper at their members. Their argument is that board members need to have full information at their disposal, in order to scrutinise the organisation thoroughly and to fulfil their legal and financial duties. But the effect can be that members can't see the wood for the trees and in reading the papers miss the really important issues that should dominate discussion. As chair you need to find a balance between the two extremes of too much and too little documentation. In particular you need to aim for papers that are concise and focus on the essential issues, and to devise short-cuts that will help members – arranging summaries of minutes of reported meetings rather than the minutes themselves, for example.

As with any group, think about how you need to prepare for the meeting. Here are some preliminaries you might consider before a board meeting:

•  welcome and prepare new members (you could give them a pack of information containing copies of the constitution, aims and objectives, recent minutes, the latest annual report and newsletters)
•  have a conversation with the chief executive and the secretary about the business to be conducted (you could ask for preparatory notes to help you chair the meeting)
•  read and make notes on the papers for the meeting

A board is a formal body, but that doesn't mean to say that its meetings always have to be chaired in a stiff, procedural way. Even in an annual general meeting, the most mechanical of events, there's room for the chair to lighten the atmosphere with pleasantries. It may be necessary to use some of the traditional rules of formal meetings summarised in sections 7.1 and 7.2 – motions, amendments, votes, points of order and so on – but only in some parts of some meetings.

However, as chair you should bear in mind at all times the legal and other responsibilities that you and other board members bear. In a charitable body, for example, if the board members are also trustees of the charity you need to be aware of the basics of charity law as it affects your work. It follows that you must reach important decisions the board takes as a charity only after proper discussion, approval and record.

You'll also be bound by the internal rules of the board. To give a mundane example, the number of absences from meetings may need to be recorded and published in the board's annual report, so that everyone can track the contributions made by individual board members.

Resorting to formality can be helpful if you're faced with important issues where opinion on the board may be badly split. Here it's crucial that you're fair to both sides in the argument, that the decision making process is transparent, and that the minutes reflect accurately and clearly what happened.

Chair: Well, we've been round this issue several times, and it seems we're fairly evenly split about what to do. I see no alternative but to take a vote. Emily, will you as Clerk to the Board count the votes with me? Our rules say that I have a casting vote in the case of a tie. Could you please put your hand up now if you're in favour of the motion? ... and against? ... abstentions?

Clerk: That's eight votes in favour, six against, one abstention.

Chair: That's my tally, too. So the motion is carried.

Following up the board meeting is normally the responsibility of the staff of the organisation: writing up and distributing minutes, fulfilling actions, preparing for the next meeting. As in other kinds of group, though, the chair's role doesn't end with the end of the meeting: you should keep in touch with the chief executive and other staff if necessary to check that the board's wishes are being carried out, and with other members of the board, especially those with formal responsibilities.

## 6.6 Representing the board and the organisation

The chair is often seen as the public face not just of the board, but of the organisation itself: the person who's interviewed on television or radio, who introduces public events such as openings, lectures or conferences, who represents the body in meetings attended by funders, politicians or those responsible for governing similar bodies. Of course, the chief executive has a similarly public-facing role, but it's the chair who will often take the lead in higher level or more publicly sensitive situations.

Like a government's ambassador, the chair champions the organisation, propagates good news, lubricates relationships with other institutions and occasionally defends the body when it comes under attack. In such a public position it helps to be experienced in public speaking and in dealing with the media, and to have good antennae for the world of politics.

The other members of the board share some of these responsibilities, and certainly the duty to act as envoys for the institution, helping to draw attention to its services and achievements. They may also be expected to help with particular external functions, such as raising funds for the organisation or making use of the networks they belong to that might not be available to the executive team. It does no harm for the chair to remind members of these duties from time to time: being on a board should mean more than just turning up to meetings. From the members' point of view, being an advocate for the board helps to enrich their involvement in the organisation's work.

If you or your fellow board members feel the need, you could arrange for appropriate training to be provided – on public speaking, for example, or appearing in the media.

## 6.7 Evaluating the board's performance

How well does the board operate? How effectively does it fulfil its functions? These are natural questions for the chair to ask. They're also ones that may be asked, or even required, by bodies that govern, fund or regulate your organisation. For companies the UK Corporate Governance Code (2012) recommends that 'the board should undertake a formal and rigorous annual evaluation of its own performance and that of its committees and individual directors'.

What's the best way of assessing the board? In most circumstances it's best to use two different methods: one to evaluate the board as a whole, the other to appraise individual members, including the chair.

An obvious way of assessing the board as a body is to require each member to complete a questionnaire, every year or two, asking questions such as:

- How well do you think the board achieves its aims, including strategy formation, organisational scrutiny and governance?
- How well does it manage its business, for example the conduct of meetings, the involvement of members, and relations between board members and the chief executive and other staff?
- How well is the board constituted? For example, does it contain the right mix of skills and knowledge? Is it representative enough?

To encourage frank responses when filling in the survey, and open discussion when the results are reported to the board, it might be worth arranging for the evaluation to be administered by a facilitator who's independent of the board and the staff. Discussion of the outcomes should concentrate on the most common shortcomings members have identified, and result in a plan of action to improve performance. This plan could lead to changes in several areas of activity: the induction and training of board members; the composition of the board; methods of recruitment to it; and the frequency and conduct of meetings.

Criticism of the board's performance in the survey should be free from personal intent, although some strictures are bound to reflect on the personal performance of the chair. However, to appraise the contribution of individual members of the board it's better to use a more informal and personal method than a questionnaire survey. A typical method is for the chair to hold an annual interview with each of the members to review their own contributions and look ahead to the next year.

A regular skills audit of board members can be helpful, to identity training needs and target gaps that need to be filled by recruitment to the board. Skills audits can also ask members what skills they feel they have developed through their work on the board.

How do you have your own performance as chair assessed? Your interviews with fellow board members, if you conduct them honestly and sensitively, may yield some clues. You could also conduct a self-assessment, using a checklist of good practice. One way of doing this is to enlist the help of a critical friend who has no connection with the board and its body but who's familiar with chairing skills, to help you explore areas where you might improve your practice.

# 7

# *Special kinds of groups and meetings*

Earlier chapters have been concerned with issues that apply to groups and meetings in general. This chapter turns to particular kinds of groups or meetings, and then to alternative methods of holding meetings.

## 7.1 Formal meetings

Older guides to chairing are concerned almost entirely with how to control formal meetings. The meetings they describe are much rarer now than they once were. But in some traditional organisations a formal style is still the rule, and even bodies that are usually informally run need to adopt more formal procedural styles from time to time, for example in order to arrive at important decisions and during annual general meetings (see section 7.2). As chair you should be aware of the basic rules of formal meetings and how to operate them. Sometimes these rules are called *standing orders* and can be very elaborate, as in the UK Parliament, where the rules of debate are included in an elaborate reference book referred to as 'Erskine May'.[19]

Most of the rules are concerned with how to make decisions – specifically, procedures for identifying proposals, adapting them, discussing them and voting on them.

Perhaps the first thing the chair needs to notice is whether the meeting has a *quorum*, that is, enough members present to reach the minimum specified by the rules. Usually a meeting that is 'inquorate', that is, with fewer than the minimum approved number present, can't make valid decisions (though it may be able to discuss matters that don't require a decision).

In a formal meeting, a proposal for action is expressed as a *motion*, a specific proposition submitted for discussion and, potentially, vote. Any eligible member of the meeting has the right to present a motion, usually in the form of a written sentence, perhaps with a number of clauses. The rules of the

---

[19] Malcolm Jack and others (eds.), *Erskine May's Treatise on the Law, Privileges, Proceedings and Usage of Parliament*, 24th ed., London: LexisNexis, 2011.

organisation may insist that the proposer gives written notice of the motion to the chair before the meeting.

As chair you must let the proposer 'move' the motion by reading out its text word for word to the members and giving reasons for supporting it. It's helpful to you if the proposer gives you a written copy at the same time, especially if the wording is long or complex. Next you should ask whether another member is willing to *second*, that is, support, the motion, either formally or by presenting arguments in favour. If no one is willing to second, then the motion 'falls' and can't be discussed. If there is a seconder, the seconder can go on to argue in favour of the motion. After that you call on other members to argue in favour or against the motion.

As well as supporting or opposing the motion, any member of the meeting has the right to propose an *amendment* to it, normally expressed explicitly as a variation (substitution, deletion or addition) of the text, and to speak in its favour provided it's been seconded. If the members of the meeting vote in favour of the amendment, the amended version becomes the *substantive motion*. If they vote against, the original motion stands and the discussion resumes. It may be that the proposer is content to accept an amendment as an improvement on the original wording: in this case there's no need for a discussion and the amendment can be accepted immediately.

In discussion, your role is to make sure that anyone who wishes to speak, whether in favour or against the motion, is able to do so, and to regulate the order of speakers. Speakers should address you rather than other members: they are said to speak 'through the Chair'. If time is pressing you might rule that members can speak only once on a single motion, or you might place a time limit on speeches, or curtail contributions that are repetitive and add nothing further to the debate. You may be able to sense if the motion is not attracting opposition. If so, call for any speaker against the motion and move towards an early vote. Before any vote is taken you should invite the proposer to reply to arguments made against the motion and to summarise the case in favour (though without introducing any further arguments).

There are formal ways a member can force the discussion to an end. Any member can propose *'that the question be put'*, indicating that discussion should cease at that point and that a vote should be taken immediately. If this proposal is carried you should put the motion to a vote at once. A more radical intervention is for a member to propose *'next business'*. This means that the meeting should immediately cease discussing the motion, without a vote, and move on to the next agenda item. Again, you should put this proposal to a vote straight away, making it clear that agreement would preclude any decision on the matter under discussion.

Any member can propose the *adjournment* of a debate. If agreed, that means the discussion is halted and postponed until a later occasion.

A member may also raise a *point of order*. This is not a remark in favour or against the motion, but a request for the chair to rule on a procedural point, for example about a breach of the standing orders or other rules of the organisation, about a speaker departing from the issue under debate, or about improper language. As chair you need to give your ruling on the basis of your best understanding and judgement. Your ruling is final and can't be challenged. Points of order should never be allowed to develop into long speeches.

| | |
|---|---|
| Federico: | A point of order, Chair. Raphael has no right to speak. He's not a member of the Council. |
| Chair: | Thank you, Federico. You're right, or at least right in part. I have the rules here, and they say that non-Council members can only speak with the approval of a majority of Council members present. Council members, would you be content for Raphael to speak? |
| All members except Federico: | Yes. |
| Chair: | Raphael, please continue. |

At the end of the discussion comes the final *vote* (there may already have been one or more earlier votes, on amendments to the original motion). You should read out the motion as it stands, clearly and in full. Then ask for a show of hands, first from those in favour of the motion, second, those against, and third, those abstaining, that is, unwilling to vote either in favour or against. All votes should be counted, if necessary by appointed counters or *tellers*, and recorded. The chair doesn't usually vote, unless the votes for and against are tied. In this case the chair, unless the rules of procedure say otherwise, has the *casting vote*. The casting vote is often assumed to be in favour of whatever is the status quo, rather than a change. If those in favour prevail, the motion is passed and becomes a *resolution*.

Formal procedures are also used for purposes other than debating motions, for example to manage the *election of officers*, where a secret ballot is normally used instead of a show of hands.

If you're involved in chairing formal meetings, you should get to know and understand these procedures. Otherwise chairing can become very difficult.

## 7.2 Annual meetings

One type of meeting where a formal style is invariable is the annual meeting. Sometimes this is called the 'annual general meeting' (AGM). Normally all eligible members of the organisation can attend, not just those who form the board or committee. Members of the public might also be present in some cases. The annual meeting is normally the sovereign institution of an organisation and is a chance for all members of a body to determine its direction, hold its officers to account, and elect new officers for the coming period. These meetings have great importance in the governance of organisations – similar to general elections in the government of a country – as they allow the current holders of power and authority to be challenged by anyone.

Most bodies have established written rules, usually as part of their constitution, for how to conduct an annual meeting. These will specify how and when members are notified of the meeting and what business will be transacted there. It's vital to make detailed preparations long before the date of the meeting, for several reasons:

- the notice of the meeting needs to be formally worded, and sent out a fixed number of days before the meeting; if the meeting is open to a wider public it will need to be advertised
- the rules will normally require standard documents to be distributed beforehand: these will include the minutes of the last annual meeting, an annual report, annual financial accounts, and nomination papers for elected positions
- these and other documents may need to be sent to other bodies, such as Companies House or the Charities Commission, and/or made available to the public
- thought may need to be given to how elections will be held

So, as chair you need to make sure that the secretary and any other people responsible for submitting documents have completed all their preparations in good time.

An agenda for an annual meeting might look like this:

1 Introduction by the chair
2 Apologies for absence
3 Minutes of the last annual meeting
4 Matters arising from the minutes
5 Presentation and adoption of the annual report
6 Presentation and adoption of the annual financial accounts
7 Appointment of auditors
8 Election of officers
9 Resolutions
10 Any other business
11 Date of next annual meeting

Depending on the type of organisation, chairs often treat the business of an annual meeting quite briskly. A well-organised and trouble-free meeting might be over within half an hour or less. Bear in mind, though, that the annual meeting could be the main fully democratic element in an organisation, and make sure that you don't stifle legitimate discussion.

Some annual meetings will require a quorum or minimum number of members to be present. If there's any danger of not achieving a quorum – or even if there's no danger but you don't wish to drag members out on a cold night for just half an hour – it might be worth organising another event to follow on from the meeting. For example, a guest speaker on a subject of wide appeal may guarantee you a respectable turnout.

The chair's introduction (1) may amount to little more than a welcome to members. Apologies for absence (2) are normally noted in the minutes. There may be provision for members who know they'll be absent to submit their votes in any election before the meeting, or to nominate a 'proxy' from among those present to vote on their behalf or represent their views. The minutes of the last annual meeting (3) and matters arising (4) are usually formal. The chair (or possibly the chief executive, if there is one) will then give an account of the main activities of the organisation since the last annual meeting (5). If a written report has been distributed, only highlights need to be mentioned. The chair should invite comments or questions from the members, and will often ask the meeting to receive or adopt the report formally.

The annual accounts (6) are usually introduced by the treasurer or director of finance, who will refer to important points, comment on the overall financial health of the organisation, and assure members that the accounts have been audited. Again, the chair should invite questions, and, asking for a proposer and seconder, invite members to vote to approve the accounts. If the accounts are audited by external accountants, it may be necessary to re-appoint them, or appoint a successor (7). If members have questions or comments, take them seriously and make sure they receive satisfactory answers.

Next come elections for officers of the organisation (8). The rules will lay down when elections take place for specific posts. Normally nominations should be made in advance, with the names of candidates, proposed and seconded by members, included with the papers for the meeting, possibly with statements or 'manifestos' written by each candidate. Some positions may be unopposed, but if there is more than one candidate for a post you'll need to preside over an election. Members normally vote in secret, on paper. The votes are collected and counted by tellers, and the results announced to the meeting. If this process is going to take some time, it may make sense to ask members to vote earlier in the meeting.

The item on resolutions (9) gives any member the right to propose a motion that requires approval by an annual meeting, for example, about raising subscriptions or changing the constitution of the organisation. The rules will often specify the areas where resolutions can be accepted as eligible for discussion.

Chair:     Now we come to item 9, 'Resolutions', and a motion to change the association's name from 'The Bankers' Syndicate' to 'The Honourable Society of Financial Servants'. It's proposed by Mr Lucre and seconded by Dr Pelf. After their speeches there will be a discussion, and then, in accordance with our constitution, I shall ask Mr Lucre to sum up before we move to a secret ballot. You'll find a copy of the motion and a ballot paper in your documents. Mr Lucre, please?

Mr Lucre:     Thank you, Chair. Now you may ask why this change is necessary ...

The final agenda item, 'Any other business' (10) shouldn't detain you long. Don't hesitate to rule out any matter irrelevant to the annual meeting. End by thanking everybody for coming, and make a point of singling out anyone who's made a particularly important contribution.

In addition to annual meetings, some organisations have a provision for holding an *extraordinary* (or *emergency*) *general meeting* (EGM) at any time of year. An EGM gives all the members a chance to discuss and decide on a matter of critical importance that can't wait for the next annual meeting. Typically an EGM will be called to consider a single proposal in the form of a written motion circulated beforehand. It can be a very serious occasion that induces strong or heated feelings – calling for a chair with a cool head and meticulous attention to detail. Who can call an EGM and in what circumstances will be set out in the constitution. It may be that a set number of members or shareholders can combine to seek one, and then the chair must organise it.

### 7.3 Conferences
A conference usually brings a substantial number of people together to learn and share knowledge (a political conference, though, is rather different). Unless decisions are to be made the chair's role in it is limited. People normally come to conferences to listen to the advertised speakers, and, to a greater or lesser extent, to take part in subsequent discussion. The less they have to put up with long speeches from the chair the better. However, your introductory and linking speeches can help set the right tone, and you'll usually have one very important 'disciplinary' role.

Most conferences are highly structured and rely on detailed preparation and strict timetabling. In recent years, less rigid variants have emerged, such as the 'unconference', where the agenda is set on the day by all the participants together, and anyone can claim a slot to speak, and the 'fishbowl', where participants join and leave a changing 'inner circle' of speakers, around which the audience sits in concentric circles.

Preparation, as always when chairing, is crucial. If you're new to the organisation or the conference, make it your business to find out about its nature and purpose – including its less tangible features, such as the degree of formality, which can affect dress and forms of address. Ask what the audience will be expecting to gain from attending. Being confident and positive is critical to being a competent conference chair, and it derives from knowing what you're doing.

Make sure that you reach the conference venue in good time. This will enable you to check that the speakers have arrived and to welcome them and put them at their ease. If one of the speakers is absent, consult with the organisers, and if necessary the other speakers, and decide how to react to the gap in the timetable.

It's always worth making sure all the speakers understand how much time they have to speak and how long the question and answer session will be. Check, too, that the room is in good order and that the sound and projection systems work properly; know where you can turn for technical help in case of trouble. If simultaneous translators are present, have a word with them about checks on equipment.

If you're giving the introduction to the conference, the main rule is to keep it brief. Welcome the delegates, and say a few words about the aim and theme of the event. A few only: your audience should already have details of the programme, including the names of speakers. Say when the audience will be able to ask questions if the programme doesn't make this clear – after each speaker or at the end of the session. Announce any 'housekeeping' instructions, such as the location of toilets, mobile phone silence, coffee and lunch details, and evacuation procedures in case of an emergency. Then stop!

Your next job is to introduce the first speaker. Again, brief is best. If the printed programme contains biographical details, don't repeat them, at least in full. Concentrate on the relevance of the speaker to the conference. If you can do so skilfully, weave in a personal or humorous thread, to help create a connection between the speaker and you and the audience – and one that can be picked up by the speaker as you hand over the microphone. Try not to steal the speaker's thunder by guessing what's going to be said.

Now comes the single most critical task of any conference chair: making sure that the speaker keeps to time. Failure here is common and can be fatal to any conference. An overrunning speaker can destroy the timetable, which in any case is likely to be tightly organised. Subsequent speakers, who find that their own time is squeezed, will be disaffected. If time for discussion is curtailed the audience will feel frustrated. Worst of all, coffee and lunch breaks may be shortened or even abolished, increasing still further the level of dissatisfaction.

Only the chair can avoid this dire situation. To do so, make sure you sit fairly close to the speakers, perhaps remaining (unobtrusively) on the platform, so that you can easily gain their attention. Give them an unambiguous warning – a visual sign or a piece of paper – five minutes before the end of the allotted time. When the time is up, insist that the speaker stops as soon as possible. This may sound brutal, but most speakers will understand, especially if you warned them before they started. Even if the speaker is irritated, the other contributors and the audience will silently thank you. Just occasionally there may be a good reason for allowing an overrun, for example if you can see the audience is entirely captivated by the speaker – but not if it means reducing time for the next speaker.

Don't switch off your attention when speakers are on their feet. Keep a wary eye open in case they need water or other helps, or the technology fails unexpectedly. And if the audience is noisy or inattentive be prepared to restore order.

When the talk is finished, wait for the applause. Lead it yourself if the audience is slow. Then thank the speaker and, if the programme allows for discussion, ask for questions and comments from the audience. Don't expect to be able to fit in too many contributions. By the time the microphone has reached the contributors, they have spoken and the speaker has responded, many minutes will have gone by. One way you can pack more into the time available is to borrow a tactic from political meetings: collect a number of brief questions from several contributors and then ask the speaker to reply to all of them in a single response. Again, the main rule is to keep an eye on the clock and not to allow discussion to overrun. Informal discussion will, of course, continue over coffee, lunch and tea breaks. These unofficial parts of a conference are often almost as important to participants as the formal presentations.

You can expect the speaker to deal well enough with most questions and comments from the conference members. After all, the opportunity to challenge is one of the points of holding a discussion. But keep an eye out for unfair or unreasonably aggressive contributors, and be prepared to intervene to discourage them. This is one good reason, by the way, for not handing over complete control of the discussion session to the speaker. Conference egotists can also be a peril. They're less interested in questioning the speaker than in drawing attention to their own superior knowledge and oratory. Again, the chair should seek, politely, to silence them once they've made their primary point.

On occasion you may find the speaker's presentation is met with complete silence, despite all your best efforts to coax contributions. In this case it's always worth keeping up your sleeve a question of your own that you can reveal if need be. It might even be the question everyone wanted to ask but which no one dared voice. Usually it will lead to other questions from the audience. Bring the session to a close by thanking the speaker again. A second round of applause should follow.

Chair: I wonder if anyone has a question for Dr Prynne? ... Or perhaps a comment on your own experience of health service reorganisation? Well, while you're thinking, let me dive in with a question of my own. Dr Prynne, can you tell us about the opposition to your ideas? Who was against you, and what were their arguments?

And so to the second speaker, and the third. Experienced chairs develop the ability to make skilful, even elegant, transitions from one speaker or one subject to the next, perhaps drawing out unnoticed themes between successive presentations. In longer conferences the burden of chairing sessions is often shared by two or more different chairs. This has the advantage that chairs can be chosen to suit the themes of different sessions.

If a panel of speakers has been assembled to answer questions from the audience and you're in the chair, make sure that all of them have a chance to express themselves. It's easy for more loquacious speakers to monopolise the time at the expense of others. Try to keep responses as brief as is reasonable in order to fit in more questions, especially if you can see that the audience is a lively one.

Unless there's a formal vote of thanks by another person, the chair brings the conference to a close by thanking the speakers, the organisers and others who deserve recognition, and sometimes by summarising the outcomes. This helps to give some coherence and shape to the variety of subjects treated during the event. It might also suggest how the work of the conference could be followed up in future. Some conferences give this summarising task to a person who isn't the chair – someone who's had the benefit of being able to concentrate on the words of the speakers and the discussion, and who can offer a personal interpretation of what's been said.

As things draw to a close, and whether or not you're responsible for the summarising, your aim should be to send the delegates away happy – or if not happy, sufficiently engaged to fill in the questionnaire on the conference at the end (most conferences will attempt to gather feedback from participants on the event, including the quality of the chairing).

### 7.4 Public meetings
Older guidebooks to chairing used to devote plenty of space to the technique of managing public, especially political, meetings. In recent decades mass political participation has declined, and

other means of communication on public matters, especially television and social media, have come to the fore. Nevertheless public meetings, though they may be less common, are still held: for example, by residents to protest against a planned development in the area, by local authorities to gauge reaction to their budget plans, by companies to consult with the public about their investment intentions.

Other meetings might not be literally public meetings, in the sense that they're open to all comers, but share some characteristics with public meetings, especially their scale. For example, you might have to chair a meeting of all the staff of your organisation, or all the members of a trade union in your area.

Presiding over a public meeting is a less predictable experience than managing a defined or known collection of people. It can cause nerves, even in a seasoned chair of smaller groups. Things can happen that you wouldn't normally expect in another kind of meeting. People may introduce unexpected subjects or arguments, others may heckle or interrupt the meeting in another way, groups may attempt to take over the meeting for their own purposes, and discussion may become so heated that it leads to less than rational language or behaviour.

The two main things to pay attention to if you're in the chair are:

- careful preparation before the meeting, including anticipating the chief challenges that might arise
- clarity, decisiveness and a firm sense of order during the meeting

If you're responsible for arranging the meeting you'll need to make a best guess about the number of people to expect, so that you can select the right size and location of venue and organise seating, refreshments, hand-outs and so on. Your 'agenda' (you may not have a formal agenda) should be as short as possible, but it needs to be attractive to an audience that will have plenty of counter-attractions. The overall subject is critical – the more topical and more local the better. It will help to be able to offer a well-known speaker: someone who's either an acknowledged expert or a well-known performer. Think about who your audience should be, and how to target them. Publicise the meeting well beforehand, through the media, flyers and posters, and other channels. Seeding social network sites can be a very effective method. Consider sending invitations to specific individuals and groups.

Think about how you're going to structure open discussion. Will there be a panel of people to deal with questions and comments? Will the invited speaker field questions? What will be your own role: will you just hold the ring, or will you be involved in the arguments in some way?

Consider what the ideal outcome of the meeting should be for you. There might be different aims in view: to gather a range of opinions from those present and judge their comparative weight; to gain assent for your proposals; to increase publicity for your activities; or to help you get elected! Then consider what will help your chosen objective, and what will hinder it. For example, if you want the public to accept the fracking site you plan to open in the neighbourhood, the last thing you need is for your meeting to be dominated by determined environmental protestors with excellent connections to local media. (But if you try to keep them out you could be accused publicly of gagging opposition or failing to engage with legitimate interests.)

If publicity is an aim, think about how you would like the event to be reported. Invite the press, television and radio, especially those you know to be friendly and fair in their coverage, but be realistic about the chances of them coming. Encourage those present to use Twitter, and issue a hashtag to focus comment. If publicity is a threat, anticipate what the main lines of criticism will be, and how you will counter them.

As always, check the practical details well before the meeting starts: the timetable, the speakers, the seating order, the presentations, the sound system, including roving microphones, and your notes on how you plan to introduce the meeting and the speakers, and to close proceedings.

When it comes to chairing the meeting itself, try to remember that you're not presiding over a committee of meeting regulars, but a heterogeneous collection of people. Don't use jargon or assume that everyone will be familiar with meeting etiquette. Make sure you've prepared a suitable 'build up' for star speakers. Don't assume that everyone will know who they are, even if they may appear to be household names. If there's a panel of speakers give them good introductions, and warn them beforehand of what their roles are (can they make speeches or do they simply answer questions, as in the BBC programme 'Question Time'?). Sit so that you can make eye-contact with them during discussion and ask them to wind up their contribution if necessary. In question and answer sessions be fair to all: keep track of everyone who wants to speak. Be firm but polite to anyone, in the audience or on the panel, who threatens to disrupt or take over the discussion. Successful heckling – jeering intended to disrupt – is an art, but so too is quelling the heckler, and usually a witty retort by the speaker will win appreciation from the audience. Only if heckling gets out of hand will the chair need to intervene. One effective way of silencing a heckler is to enlist the goodwill of the audience in your wish to see order restored. Another is to deflate the heckler with your own native wit – though you may feel this could reduce your gravitas. And not everyone is blessed with the wit of the eighteenth-century politician John Wilkes, who replied to a heckler's jeer, 'Vote for you? I'd sooner vote for the Devil' with the retort, 'And if your friend decides against standing, can I count on your vote?'

| The Chief: | Friends and fellow brigands, I have a proposal to make to this meeting ... |
| The Anarchist: | [rising] A point of order, Mendoza— |
| Mendoza: | [forcibly] No, by thunder: your last point of order took half an hour. Besides, Anarchists don't believe in order. |

The Anarchist: [mild, polite but persistent: he is, in fact, the respectable looking elderly man in the celluloid collar and cuffs] That is a vulgar error. I can prove—

Mendoza: Order, order.

The others: [shouting] Order, order. Sit down. Chair! Shut up.

George Bernard Shaw, *Man and Superman* (1903), Act 3.

A more difficult challenge than heckling, especially when the topic of the meeting is highly contentious, is when tempers flare during a discussion, between individuals or groups of individuals. It's one thing to recognise and tolerate genuine and deep-held conflicts of view, expressed with honesty and passion. It's quite another to allow people to be abusive or offensive, to cow opponents with aggressive interruptions, or to silence others through making long-winded, repetitious speeches. This is when the chair should step in, restrain the offenders and restore calm to the discussion. You may need to exert some firmness, but by intervening decisively at the right time you'll prevent a difficult situation from getting worse. It can be helpful to remind everyone that they've come together to share views and that barracking prevents this. It may also help to appeal to the audience's sense of decency and fair play.

If you've significant messages to give to the meeting – for example, about the importance of becoming a member of your society – don't leave them to the very end, but insert them into your remarks throughout the meeting. But when you do reach the end, make it a resounding one that will linger with the audience. Depending on the nature of the event, you might want everyone present to have left their names and contact details with you, or at least to take away a leaflet or membership form. Try to avoid a nondescript or downbeat conclusion. Those present shouldn't feel that they might have spent their time more productively by staying at home. They should feel enthused, and on your side.

## 7.5 Appointment panels

The meeting of an appointment panel is unusual in that its consequences can be serious and long-term. They can also involve employment and equality law and regulation. One of the most curious features of what is still the basic recruitment method, the job interview, is that an encounter lasting no more than an hour may acquire someone who will be a valuable and reliable staff member or board member for thirty years – or saddle an organisation with a troublemaker who will create discord and waste resources for a similar period. There are many other sources of guidance on interviewing practices, but what follows concentrates on the role of the chair of a panel.

Today organisations have a range of different methods to choose from when recruiting: application forms; trawling and sifting by head-hunters; assessment centres; psychometric, personality and technical tests; presentations; and informal meetings with staff. The interview, though, has retained its dominant position as the main determinant of how suitable shortlisted candidates are. If you happen to be in the chair when the interview takes place, whether for a job in an organisation or a position on its governing body, what are the essential things for you to remember?

As always when chairing, planning is critical. Do your personal homework, by reading the applications and becoming familiar with the organisation's rules and procedures for appointments. If necessary, contact the human resources department for advice. On the day, convene the panel well before the first candidate is due to arrive. Make sure all the panel members are clear about the nature of the post. Run through the skills and knowledge that a candidate needs to demonstrate. Some of these will be obvious from the application form and other prior evidence. Others will need to be gleaned during the course of the interview.

Next, decide what questions to ask, who'll ask them, and in what order. To maintain consistency and fairness the same primary questions should be directed to each candidate. Select

137

questions that will elicit useful information to help you match what the candidate offers against the needs of the post.

Decide how the panel members are going to record their notes and score the candidates on each question. Ask if the other panel members have any queries, or whether the human resources department representative has any additional information of relevance, for example about equality and diversity requirements. Finally, check that the immediate environment is satisfactory, including presentation equipment and water for the candidate.

The first candidate is shown in, or you may go to collect them so that you can begin cultivating a friendly atmosphere on the way to the interview room. It's your job to make sure the interview is a success, that is, that the panel finds out what it needs to about the candidate, and the candidate is able to judge the suitability of the organisation. Your first and most basic task, once you've made the introductions and explained the format of the interview, is to put the candidate at ease. Don't rush straight into the set questions, but begin with some easy conversation and a simple, open question to get the candidate started and in as relaxed a state as is possible in the situation. Some people feel that higher tension and formality give a chance to test a candidate's nerve, but what you should want is for the candidates to be able to show their best, and nerves are unlikely to help.

If the candidate is giving a presentation to the panel at the start, check that any equipment is working properly, and keep an eye on the clock: it's important that no candidate is allowed more time than the others.

Next, the questioning. The panel members will ask their allotted standard questions, but they should be entitled to ask supplementary or probing questions to follow up on the candidate's initial reply or in response to points made in the initial presentation. Make sure that no panel member exceeds the time allotted at the expense of others, and of course that they don't ask questions that are illegal or contrary to the organisation's own recruitment rules. Don't allow panel members to cut in on one another to ask supplementary questions, as this can unnerve and disorientate the candidate. Keep a note, on paper or in your head, of the topics covered, and when the panel members have finished ask any further questions that might be needed to elicit information that hasn't yet emerged. Finally, give the candidate time to ask questions, and either answer them yourself or turn to one of the other panel members.

All this time the panel members should be evaluating how well the candidates demonstrate the skills and knowledge needed for the post, and noting their scores and comments on paper. And, of course, the candidate will be weighing up whether working for your organisation would be a good idea – another reason for the chair to take pains to ensure that the interview experience is positive for everyone.

When the last candidate has left the room your role as chair comes into its own. Assessing the merits of the candidates and making the appointment are – or should be – complex processes that call for care and sensitivity. Often this stage is rushed, with decisions reached on the basis of inadequate discussion. Sometimes irrational reactions to a candidate's manner or expression can colour judgement. Interviewing is an exhausting business, demanding total concentration for hours, and tiredness can overwhelm the panel members if they've interviewed more than a few candidates. It's up to you to avoid this and ensure that the panel explores all the relevant information they have before coming to a verdict, which must be seen to be fair, evidence-based, and not discriminatory. There are several methods and techniques you could use:

- ask panel members to declare any relationship with the candidate
- take a break before the assessment begins: this will offer an opportunity for each panel member to stretch their legs, and also to gather thoughts and weigh up evidence
- make it clear whether or not you'll offer your own opinion on the candidates or 'hold the ring' without expressing a

preference: your choice will be determined largely by the circumstances
- remind the panel they should evaluate each candidate strictly against the published list of skills and knowledge required for the post, and on the basis of *all* the information they have – not just the interview, but the application form, feedback from prior presentations or meetings, and any other evidence except supposition or hearsay
- agree on the method for discussing the candidates: will you go round the table, taking each candidate in turn?
- score individually, then combine the panel's agreed scores for each candidate, decide on weighting of the different criteria, and come to an overall judgement
- consider asking the panel members to postpone a verdict in the initial round of assessment, then ask for provisional judgements before another discussion
- once a consensus seems to be emerging around a particular candidate, think about adopting the role of a devil's advocate in order to test whether the consensus is based on firm evidence, or on sentiment and assumption
- you might need to take repeated 'tours' round the table before you're sure that all are agreed on a winner and secure in their judgement

A verdict on the successful candidate is not quite the end of your work. There'll be several other decisions to be taken:

- Will there be a report of the process and, if so, who will compile it?
- How will any details of the appointment that remain uncertain, like its starting date, be arranged?
- Who will contact the candidates about the result, and offer feedback on their performance if they choose to hear it?
- How will you deal with any reserve candidates that you consider appointable?

Don't forget to thank your panel members at the end. If they've done their job well they fully deserve your gratitude.

## 7.6 Quasi-judicial meetings: disciplinary and grievance hearings

Some of the most challenging meetings to chair are those sharing features with judicial proceedings. Usually these take place in an employment setting. Common examples are meetings to hear disciplinary cases, where an employee is charged with a serious offence in the workplace, and grievance hearings, where an employee alleges unfair treatment by the management of the organisation or by another staff member.

The chair of hearings has to take special care in these cases. They may start as internal hearings within the organisation, but if they don't reach a definitive conclusion they can easily lead later to external, judicial investigations by a higher authority, such as an industrial tribunal or a court of law. Here attention may focus on the fairness of the original hearing – in other words, how the chair conducted its procedures.

If you're the chair of a board you may be the final stage of an appeals procedure, that is, if it extends beyond the original hearing. In this case you should avoid taking any part in that hearing, so that your position later on will not be prejudiced.

In preparing for and conducting the hearing you need to pay close attention to the established procedural rules that apply to the hearing, and to the demands of fairness and natural justice.

Read and become thoroughly familiar with the regulations that the organisation has in place for the kind of hearing you're presiding over. They're likely to be detailed, specific and clear. Make sure you and everyone involved sticks to these rules throughout the proceedings. A failure to do so may in extreme cases invalidate the hearing. So important are these rules that if you find that they don't exist in the organisation in question you should probably think twice before agreeing to chair the hearing.

Written rules, though, are the beginning and not the end of being fair, which is your chief concern as chair. They can't

141

legislate for every circumstance. You also need to bear in mind your more general duty to demonstrate that you're scrupulous in your concern to be fair to all sides, that you give everyone concerned an equal opportunity to be heard, and that you don't discriminate against anyone – or allow anyone else to discriminate. You may find it helpful to consult generic codes of practice in disciplinary cases, such as the code published by ACAS.[20]

If you do adhere to the written procedures and abide by the common rules of fairness you should have nothing to fear from any subsequent investigation of how your hearing was conducted – assuming that an accurate and detailed record of what happened has been taken and agreed.

As ever, you should make sure that you've re-read and understood all the documentation thoroughly before the date of the hearing.

Exactly how *disciplinary hearings* are organised will depend on the relevant regulations, but here is one pattern:

*Welcome and introductions*
Those present may include the staff member who is the subject of the disciplinary procedure, a companion of the staff member (possibly a trade union representative), the panel members who will adjudicate, an 'investigating officer' or prosecutor who presents the charges, a note-taker unconnected with the case, and a member of the human resources team. The chair should confirm that all the preliminary procedures have been followed correctly, that everyone understands the procedures in the meeting, the roles of everyone present, the documentation provided, and the possible outcomes.

---

[20]ACAS, *Disciplinary and Grievance Procedures*, Norwich: TSO, 2009. http://www.acas.org.uk/media/pdf/k/b/Acas_Code_of_Practice_1_on _disciplinary_and_grievance_procedures-accessible-version-Jul-2012.pdf

## Presentation of the charges and evidence

The investigating officer next details the charges brought against the staff member, introducing documentary evidence and, if necessary, calling witnesses. The chair should give the staff member and the panel members ample opportunity to interrogate the investigating officer and the witnesses, and to question the documentary evidence.

## Presentation by the staff member

The staff member then presents the defence case, again calling witnesses and citing evidence in the documentation. The chair should give the investigating officer and panel members the chance to ask questions of the staff member and any witnesses.

## Discussion and adjudication by the panel

The chair reminds the staff member about the next steps after the conclusion of the hearing, including any right to appeal. Then those concerned with the 'prosecution' and 'defence' withdraw. The panel members consider all the arguments and evidence presented to them, and judge whether the charges against the staff member are valid. The chair should let the panel members have as much time as they need to reach their decision, taking breaks in the discussion as required.

## Summary and conclusion

The chair summarises the conclusion of the panel's deliberations and the next steps, and thanks the panel members and note-taker for their work. When they're ready the chair later approves the official notes of the hearing.

*Grievance hearings* will have a similar kind of procedure, except that of course the staff member or representative is in the position of 'prosecutor'.

## 7.7 Facilitating

Facilitating meetings is quite different from chairing them, and calls for different, or rather, additional skills.

Facilitation means 'easing' a process or solution. The emphasis is less on control and firm direction than on supporting the members, or acting as an intellectual midwife, coaxing and inducing ideas from them. The meeting is likely to be devoted to a single subject, usually a significant and complex one that lacks one obvious 'solution', like the future direction of the organisation, how to solve a difficult conflict, or where to find new sources of support. The facilitator's role is to encourage productive ideas, seek consensus, and structure the outcomes so that the group members can put them to work on their own. In discussion, dialogue rather than debate is the aim.

Who's the best person to act as facilitator? The group's own chair might be an obvious choice, but even if the chair is recognised as unbiased and open-minded the group members may be too accustomed to the chair's techniques and ways of working. Other trusted members of the group could take on the role, especially if they've received training in facilitation methods. But often the choice falls on an external expert facilitator. Outsiders can bring not only long experience of facilitation techniques but also a valuable distance from the group's assumptions and habitual ways of thinking. They may need to learn the context and 'language' of the group, but will normally have little difficulty if they receive a thorough briefing beforehand.

A facilitator is in charge of the meeting for most of its length and should possess all the general skills of a chair: listening, empathising, leading and so on. But you'll need some additional characteristics and skills:

- You need to maintain strict neutrality. A good chair, of course, will not normally take sides, but a chair often has a stake in the outcome of a discussion, whereas a facilitator has no interest in the nature of the group's decisions.

- The process of discussion and decision is crucial, and so is participation. As facilitator you need to involve all members equally in the process. You also need to get the best out of each one: to encourage everyone to think in considered, creative and possibly unusual ways, and to express themselves so as to engage the understanding and imagination of their fellows.
- You're searching for consensus and agreement. So throughout the session you should be on the lookout for bridges between different arguments, and be ready to summarise points of connection. On the other hand, you need to probe and challenge what participants say, so that they avoid reaching premature conclusions that have escaped thorough examination.

To achieve good results as a facilitator it helps to have a range of techniques that you can use, depending on the situation, to help the generation of ideas, clarify and analyse concepts, and build consensus. Even an expert chair may not be familiar with these methods and when to use them, and a specialist course in facilitating may be necessary to be able to master them. They include:

- Icebreaking: a technique for introducing people who may not know one another, and for stimulating creative juices. It often takes the form of a short question and answer dialogue between pairs of members on a subject other than the topic of group discussion. The results are then reported briefly to the whole group. The facilitator should get to know people's names at an early stage in the session (name badges or cards will help).
- Role play: a way of encouraging members to see the situation from different perspectives. A common example is Edward de Bono's 'Six Thinking Hats' method, which asks participants to assume a temporary 'hat' or type of enquiry or opinion, for example 'white' for eliciting or providing

information, or 'red' for expressing a gut emotional reaction.

- Brainstorming: a way of generating and documenting a 'pile' of ideas very quickly in the open group, within a set time limit. Exploration and criticism of these are deliberately postponed till later.
- Nominal group technique: here each group member develops a solution to the problem independently and silently, then presents it to the whole group. Once duplicate ideas have been amalgamated the group ranks those remaining. Often this method produces more ideas than are generated in open discussion.
- Small group work: often people will be readier to produce ideas more rapidly if they discuss them in pairs or small groups rather than in a larger setting. Try splitting the group into different smaller groups on different occasions to ring the changes on combinations of people. Each time give the groups specific questions to answer. At the end, pool, cluster and analyse the answers. If you want everyone to participate fully, around six people per group seems to be a maximum.
- Action-based work: techniques that require work rather than just oral contributions from participants. This method can be useful when prioritising or voting on a list of possibilities. Many kinds of materials can be pressed into play: sticky notes, flipcharts or plastic building bricks.

Whether and in what circumstances you should use these will depend on your sense – and here an empathetic ability is helpful – of how the members will react to them. Some people may be instinctively uncomfortable with role play if they haven't encountered the technique before. Seasoned members may treat the prospect of half an hour's fixing sticky notes to walls with a cynical disdain.

A lot of thought needs to be put into planning these, particularly about which techniques and topics will most stimulate the people involved and best suit the circumstances, and how you're going to decide who should be in which groups.

Splitting the whole group into sub-groups creates a dilemma at the end of their work. Do you attempt to collect and summarise all the discussions so that everyone can hear what's been said, or not? If you do decide to have a 'report back' session, make sure it's brief and not repetitious.

Lack of time should be less of a problem in facilitated sessions: you might have a whole day available, possibly away from your normal location. Make sure that there are plenty of refreshments in the room, and timetable enough breaks. Be patient: it will take time to tease out new ideas and explore their potentials and pitfalls – and to build a real consensus, which is the facilitator's ultimate aim. As views begin to coalesce around a set of proposals your role is to check that they've been subjected to enough scrutiny. Summarise them and repeat them back to the members. If necessary, challenge members to defend their positions. Check, too, that the decisions have general support among the members. And finally, even if the discussion has been mainly theoretical and general, try by the end of the session to get the members to formulate their proposals in as concrete a way as possible, so that once you've gone they can start putting them into action without revisiting earlier arguments.

## 7.8 Bilingual and multilingual meetings

First-language English speakers tend to be monoglots. They seldom give thought to the linguistic needs of those for whom English is a second, or non-preferred, language. But in some meetings language is a serious consideration, and the sensitive chair should be aware of its importance.

In meetings that are conducted entirely in English you should be conscious that for some participants English may not be their first language. Their comprehension of spoken English, and their fluency when speaking it, may vary. Satisfy yourself that they're able to follow what you and others say, and that they're not inhibited from making contributions to discussion by a lack of linguistic confidence. And if you're chairing a formal presentation by non-first language English speakers, be ready to help them out if they find accents or expressions from subsequent questioners hard to understand.

Chairing bilingual meetings can be more of a challenge if you're not used to them, but with practice it becomes almost second nature. They're common in overseas countries, and, in the UK, in Wales, where statute or policy may dictate that both Welsh and English can be used equally during the course of a meeting. It's assumed here that Welsh is the non-English language, but the same comments apply to other languages.

Normally a simultaneous translator will be present to translate Welsh contributions into English, and non-Welsh speakers will listen on headphones.

Your introduction is crucial: remember that it's the chair who sets the linguistic register of the meeting. There are several essential steps you'll need to take:

- before starting the meeting ask the translator and headphone users to check that the translation system is working properly
- welcome members in both languages
- make it clear that participants are welcome to contribute in either language

If you're a Welsh speaker then use Welsh yourself for at least half of what you say, so that Welsh-speaking members, who may include learners, will feel confident enough to use the language themselves when they contribute. If you're not a Welsh speaker, counteract what might become a tendency for English to become the default language by using Welsh phrases you're comfortable with or by repeating your invitation to use Welsh. Your overall aim should be to encourage members to make active use of their right to use Welsh, and not to feel that the presence of English-only speakers is an inhibition.

In the course of discussion it's normal for a question to be answered in the language of the questioner, though again it would be acceptable to respond in Welsh to a question or comment in English if you're anxious to avoid the danger of English dominating. Simultaneous translation is a taxing and tiring job: if meetings threaten to be prolonged, take pity on the translators and give them a break!

Documentation associated with the meeting should be in bilingual form: the agenda, minutes and papers, screen-based presentations, and hand-outs prepared by the speakers.

At the end of the meeting always make your final remarks in both languages, and make sure you thank the translator.

## 7.9 Remote meetings: teleconferences and videoconferences

Meetings are not always face-to-face. Sometimes it simply isn't possible to bring everyone together physically, for example if they happen to be in different cities or on different continents. And even if it's possible it may not make economic or environmental sense for people to travel from different places to a central location for an encounter that will only last an hour or two. Remote meetings are common, both internally within a geographically distributed company or other organisation, and also to link separate organisations or individuals.

There are two media to consider if you're planning a remote meeting: audio or audiovisual. Both are possible using either dedicated networks or the open internet.

The simplest and cheapest way of arranging a small-scale internal voice-only meeting is through the organisation's own telephone network. This allows additional voices to join, and several people clustered in a location can participate through a phone operating in speaker mode.

For larger-scale meetings and where sound quality is important it's best to use a dedicated facility. Several participants can share in a single conversation through a telephone conference, often abbreviated to 'teleconference'. Many telecom companies offer conference facilities. Typically participants use a 'conference bridge' provided by the company: they dial a prearranged phone number and join the conversation in turn through a special, prearranged code. If there are several people in one of the locations they can all speak and be heard through a single 'spider' placed in the centre of the table.

Similarly, in an audiovisual meeting or 'videoconference', different locations are connected using an external service. Each location will usually have a studio large enough to accommodate up to twenty or so people and equipped with technologies both to control the meeting and to allow the sharing of documents or presentations. A centralised service is used for booking sessions. Research should easily identify companies that offer dedicated videoconferencing systems.

As internet capacities and speeds have increased many people now use the internet rather than dedicated systems to hold their meetings. The 'Voice over Internet Protocol' (VoIP) allows audio and audiovisual conversations to take place on the internet without resorting to the public switched telephone network (PSTN). A VoIP service typically operates on all kinds of device, including laptops, tablets and smart-phones. Many devices have cameras and microphones built in, so all you need to start is the service's software and someone to speak to. Often the basic service is free, but to arrange a multi-node meeting you may need to pay.

For all their convenience and economy remote methods have obvious disadvantages for meetings compared with face-to-face discussions, especially for the chair. Technologies can fail, at the start or halfway through the meeting. It's hard to keep track of all the participants – even to be certain whether they're still present. The normal non-verbal clues you rely on – for example, to sense when a member is keen to intervene – are absent or harder to discern. For these reasons there are three rules to remember if you're contemplating using a teleconference or videoconference.

First, it's usually best if you can to avoid videoconferencing or teleconferencing as a medium for a group's *first* meeting, unless the members already know one another well. The first meeting is crucial for any new group, as an opportunity for members to get to know one another and start to build the trust and sense of connection that are needed for the group to succeed. It's hard to begin that process if you're on your own in a remote studio, with other members scattered in other locations. Even those who are clustered in a single place may have little chance to hold informal conversations.

Second, remote meetings are not well suited to complex discussions, especially about relatively theoretical matters. If you're looking for a rich exchange of ideas from a wide range of voices interacting in a fluid and sophisticated way, it's far easier to achieve success face-to-face. Where remote methods can work well and efficiently is in regular meetings whose purpose is mainly to transact standard kinds of business or make routine operational decisions.

Third, make sure that you're familiar with how the technologies you're using work: how to register or dial in, how to operate any dashboard or screen, how to ensure everyone can see accompanying documents or slides. And if possible arrange to have a competent technician on hand in case of failed connections or other problems. Testing connections before the start of the meeting is always a good precaution.

Chairing teleconferences and videoconferences calls for extra levels of concentration and attentiveness. You can't see all or most of the other members – or, if you can, you may not be able to see them clearly enough to pick up their eye contacts or other signals easily. So you need to check with members more often than you would need to do in a face-to-face meeting, to discover whether they wish to speak, to confirm their assent to proposals, or even to satisfy yourself that they're still there: remote members can silently disappear in the middle of a meeting if their network connections fail.

When planning the meeting, ensure that everyone has received the instructions for joining the call, and a list of everyone participating. Arrive early and test the technologies, including sound levels and camera angles. Encourage people to frame themselves sensibly in the camera so that everyone can be seen and that they are as visible as possible. Don't let a single participant appear as a dot in the middle of the picture when they could move into close-up.

When introducing the meeting you should do a 'roll call' of everyone taking part. You might need to emphasise some points of etiquette. For example, members new to videoconferencing often don't realise that shuffling papers or tapping pens close to the microphone may sound thunderous to members in other locations. One way to avoid this is for members to mute their microphones except when speaking themselves. When speaking, especially for the first time, it's useful to begin by saying, for example, 'This is Eric speaking, from Accounts...'

You may also need to control the discussion in a more organised way than you would need to with everyone gathered in a single room. For example, you should ask members to speak in turn rather than across one another. It happens quite often that two people start to speak at exactly the same time, and you should be prepared to intervene to give preference to one of them. You also need to beware of the danger that the location with the larger number of participants will start to have a face-to-face conversation itself, with the remote people becoming observers rather than participants. The ultimate danger is of partial or complete loss of your connection. If it can't be re-established, you should know how to finish the business using a different medium.

If you have to pay very close attention during a remote meeting, so do the other members, so it's wise to restrict the length of the meeting to, say, an hour or an hour and a half – and if a longer meeting is unavoidable, make sure that you have a break in the middle.

# 8

## *Looking back and looking forward*

What does it feel like to have chaired a group and its meetings successfully over a period of time?

Unless you're deluding yourself and you've actually been a poor chair – some of the assessment techniques mentioned in Chapter 6 should help allay that suspicion – you'll be able to look back with some satisfaction and conclude that:

- the group has begun to achieve the objectives set for it at the start
- ... and it has kept to the timetable it was given
- all the group's members have worked in harmony, combining their different strengths, contributing fully to the group
- ... and developing a spirit of pride in achievement and thirst for future success
- the group's parent body or its public acknowledges the group's effectiveness
- ... and recognises the values of its achievements
- you as chair have played a critical part in the group's success
- ... and you've drawn personal knowledge and enjoyment from the experience

Unsurprisingly, repeated experience of chairing tends to sharpen the various skills involved. The more chairing situations you encounter, the easier you find it to know how to react to a difficult issue or person. Presiding over small or medium-sized groups gives you the confidence to cope with larger gatherings, including public meetings. And gradually you cease to be anxious at all, and begin to relish the prospect of chairing a new group, even in an unfamiliar field of activity.

You'll find, though, that there's always something new to learn as chair. Thinking about your own practice and observing how other chairs operate will inevitably suggest new ways of making groups work more effectively and producing better results from time spent in meetings.

Chairing is a sought-after skill. Most people are quick to appreciate the value of someone who has the ability to orchestrate a varied group of people to produce a successful result, without unnecessary conflict and waste of time. If you can show that you almost always operate effectively in the chair, people and organisations will start to turn to you to chair other groups and meetings. And so a virtuous circle evolves: the more experienced you become, the more you're trusted to preside over new groups, and the more this additional experience further expands your range of skills.

It's easy to overlook your experience of chairing when you prepare your *curriculum vitae*, but in their recruiting most employers will note with approval a record of experience in the field, and most voluntary organisations looking for suitable people to chair their boards or committees will be even more eager to secure the services of a proven chair. What's more, if you've been a successful chair, you've also shown that you possess the skills needed for chairing: concentration on achieving objectives, tact and patience, analytical and listening skills, good communication, time management, conflict resolution and leadership – all of them invaluable in almost any kind of employment.

Perhaps, in time, your expertise will become so well tuned that some people cease to notice that the meetings you chair progress with practised smoothness or that the groups you manage always deliver what's asked of them. But there will always be discerning people who, at the end of a meeting, will make a point of 'thanking the chair' – and they'll mean it.

# A chairing checklist:
# 10 'dos' and 'don'ts'

1 Do your homework
   - research the group: its business and aims, its members and operation
   - understand your own role and expectations
   - plan meetings carefully, especially their environment
   - prepare yourself: re-read, reflect, anticipate

2 Listen with understanding
   - observe how the group's members behave and interact
   - learn how to inhabit the mental space of other people
   - don't let your attention wander during meetings
   - keep a clear head and think on your feet

3 Be fair and consistent
   - treat all the members equally and with respect: don't have favourites
   - don't take sides in arguments in an unjust way
   - develop trust between members, and nurture their trust in you

4 Keep your eye on the objective
   - never lose sight of the group's main goals
   - don't be deflected by the irrelevant, the trivial and the mischievous
   - keep a close eye on time passing
   - make sure that clear decisions are reached

157

5 Intervene with a purpose
  • don't let meetings drift: lead, don't be led
  • defuse situations that threaten to get out of hand
  • beware of groupthink, false consensus and false compromise
  • ensure you're thoroughly familiar with the group's rules

6 Challenge and summarise
  • test the understanding and agreement of the members
  • sum up the arguments during and at the end of discussions
  • make sure everyone understands decisions and what will happen to them

7 Follow up
  • check that agreed actions have been carried out
  • prepare for the next steps and the next meeting
  • represent the group effectively and report on its work

8 Get on with your chief executive
  • develop an understanding of who does what
  • try to develop a personal 'chemistry' that works for both of you
  • don't hide things from the chief executive, and don't let yourself be surprised
  • keep a certain degree of distance and don't stand by if problems occur

9 Be human
  • get to know the members personally
  • be unstinting in your the use of words like 'welcome' and 'thank you'
  • exert your authority lightly
  • communicate with members outside meetings

10 Keep learning
- watch how others chair groups and meetings
- observe yourself, and be critical of your own performance
- ask your members how you're doing

# Further reading

**General**

Julie-Ann Amos, *Making Meetings Work*, 2nd ed., Oxford: How To Books, 2002.

Alan Barker, *Making Meetings Work: A Practical Guide*, London: Industrial Society, 1993.

Alan Barker, *How to Manage Meetings*, 2nd ed., London: Kogan Page, 2011.

Paul Brown and Fiona Hackett, *Managing Meetings*, London: Fontana, 1990.

Roz Burch, *Chairing Meetings: A Training Manual*, Loughborough: Sahara, 2006.

Michael Doyle and David Straus, *How to Make Meetings Work: The New Interactive Method*, New York: Wyden Books, 1976.

Tim Hindle, *Managing Meetings*, London: Dorling Kindersley, 1998.

Philip Hodgson and Jane Hodgson, *Effective Meetings*, London: Century Business, 1992.

Greville Janner, *Janner on Chairing*, London: Gower, 1989.

Greville Janner, *Janner on Meetings*, London: Gower, 1986.

Local Government Association, *Chairing Skills: Councillor Workbook*, London: Local Government Association, 2012. http://www.boston.gov.uk/CHttpHandler.ashx?id=7659& p=0

Karen Mannering, *Making Meetings Work*, London: Hodder Education, 2011.

John Marsh and Madeleine Sumsion, *Chairing Meetings*, Winchester: South East Employers, 1998.

*Meetings, Bloody Meetings: How to Make Meetings More Productive*, [video], London: Video Arts, 2012.

Consuelo O'Connor, *The View from the Chair: The Art of Chairing Meetings,* Ballivor, Co. Meath: Zircon, 1994.

Howell Parry, *Meetings*, London: Croner, 1991.

Duncan Peberdy and Jane Hammersley, *Brilliant Meetings: What to Know, Do and Say to Have Fewer, Better Meetings,* Harlow: Prentice Hall, 2009.

Malcolm Peel, *How to Make Meetings Work*, London: Kogan Page, 1988.

Sophie Petit-Zeman, *How to Be an Even Better Chair: Sensible Advice from the Public and Charity Sectors*, Harlow: Pearson Prentice Hall Business, 2006.

Barbara J. Streibel, *Plan and Conduct Effective Meetings: 24 Steps to Generate Meaningful Results*, New York: McGraw-Hill, 2007.

Sue Ward, *A-Z of Meetings,* London: Pluto, 1985.

Graham Willcocks and Steve Morris, *Making Meetings Work in a Week*, London: Hodder & Stoughton, 2000.

## Formal meetings

Walter Citrine, *The ABC of Chairmanship*, 4th ed., edited by Michael Cannell and Norman Citrine, London: NCLC, 1982.

Madeleine Cordes and others (eds.), *Shackleton on the Law and Practice of Meetings*, 12th ed., London: Sweet and Maxwell, 2011.

Wal Hannington, *Mr Chairman! A Short Guide to the Conduct and Procedure of Meetings*, London: Lawrence and Wishart, 1950.

Malcolm Jack and others (eds.), *Erskine May's Treatise on the Law, Privileges, Proceedings and Usage of Parliament*, 24th ed., London: LexisNexis, 2011.

Gordon R. Wainwright, *Meetings and Committee Procedure*, London: Hodder and Stoughton, 1987.

## Boards

Neville Bain and Roger Barker, *The Effective Board: Building Individual and Board Success*, London: Kogan Page, 2010.

C. Cornforth and C. Edwards, *Good Governance: Developing Effective Board-Management Relations in Public and Voluntary Organisations*, London: Chartered Institute of Management Accountants, 1998.

Hilary Douglas, *What Makes a Great Chair in the Public Sector?* London: Praesta Partners LLP, [n.d.] www.praesta.co.uk/_resource/_upload/190551211.pdf

Patrick Dunne, *Running Board Meetings: Tips and Techniques for Getting the Best from Them*, 3rd ed., London: Kogan Page, 2005.

Financial Reporting Council, *Guidance on Board Effectiveness*, London: FRC, 2011. https://www.frc.org.uk/getattachment/c9ce2814-2806-4bca-a179-e390ecbed841/Guidance-on-Board-Effectiveness.aspx

Financial Reporting Council, *The UK Corporate Governance Code*, London: FRC, 2012. https://www.frc.org.uk/Our-Work/Publications/Corporate-Governance/UK-Corporate-Governance-Code-September-2012.pdf

Penelope Gibbs, *A Marriage Made in Heaven? The Relationship between Chairs and Chief Executives in Charities*, London: Association of Chief Executives of Voluntary Organisations, 2011. http://www.cloresocialleadership.org.uk/userfiles/documents/Research%20reports/2010/Research,%20Penelope%20Gibbs,%20FINAL.pdf

John Harper, *Chairing the Board: A Practical Guide to Activities and Responsibilities*, rev. ed., London: Kogan Page, 2005.

Andrew Kakabadse, *Leading the Board: The Six Disciplines of World Class Chairmen*, Basingstoke: Palgrave Macmillan, 2008.

*What Makes a Great Board Chair? 215 of the UK's Top Directors give their views*, London: The Change Partnership, [2004]. http://www.mairieastwood.com/wp-content/uploads/2013/08/What-makes-a-great-Board-Chair-copy.pdf

## Conferences
David Seekings with John Farrer, *How to Organize Effective Conferences and Meetings*, 7th ed., London: Kogan Page, 1999, Chapter 14: 'The art of chairing a conference'.

## Interviewing
Jane Newell Brown, *The Complete Guide to Recruitment*, London: Kogan Page, 2011.

Sandra Bunting, *The Interviewer's Handbook: Successful Interviewing Techniques for the Workplace*, London: Kogan Page, 2005.

Margaret Dale, *A Manager's Guide to Recruitment and Selection*, 2nd ed., London: Kogan Page, 2003.

## Disciplinary and grievance hearings
*Discipline and Grievances at Work: the ACAS guide*, London: ACAS, 2011. http://www.acas.org.uk/media/pdf/s/o/Acas-Guide-on-discipline-and-grievances_at_work_%28April_11%29-accessible-version-may-2012.pdf

## Facilitating
Esther Cameron, *Facilitation Made Easy: Practical Tips to Improving Meetings and Workshops*, 3rd ed., London: Kogan Page, 2005.

John Heron, *The Complete Facilitator's Handbook*, London: Kogan Page, 1999.

Christine Hogan, *Practical Facilitation: A Toolkit of Techniques*, London: Kogan Page, 2003.

Jenny Rogers, *Facilitating Groups*, London: Open UP/McGraw Hill Education, 2010.

## Bilingual meetings

*Guide for Chairing Bilingual Meetings Effectively*. [Fredericton]:
    Government of New Brunswick, 2011.
    http://www2.gnb.ca/content/dam/gnb/Departments/ohr-
    brh/pdf/tk/TK-Guide_Bilingual_Meetings.pdf

## Videoconferencing

Rob Bristow, Mark Barratt and Theresa Millar, *Using
    Videoconferencing and Collaboration Technology to Reduce
    Travel and Carbon Emissions*, London: Jisc, [n.d.].
    http://www.jisc.ac.uk/guides/using-videoconferencing-and-
    collaboration-technology-to-reduce-travel-and-carbon-emissi
    ons

# Index

absentees from meetings 46-7, 62, 92, 114, 126, 129
ACAS 142
accountability of groups 24, 93
accounts, annual 126
acoustics of meetings 51-2, 152
  see also microphones
action-based group work 146
action points 35, 47, 64, 65, 67, 68, 90, 92, 93
acumen 13-14
adjournment of debates and meetings 84, 123
advertising meetings 125, 134
advisory boards 97
advocacy role of chairs and boards 111-12, 115
agendas 15, 44-9, 62, 78
  annual meetings 125-8
  boards 104, 112-13
  public meetings 133-4
aggression, in meetings 82-3, 136
agreement see consensus in meetings
aims see objectives
ambassadorial role of chairs and boards 111-12, 115
amendments
  to minutes 65, 92-3
  to motions 122
annual accounts 126
annual (general) meetings (AGMs) 60, 121, 124-8
  company boards 104
annual reports 104, 126

'any other business' 48, 62, 68-9, 127
apologies for absence 46-7, 62, 114, 126
appeals procedures 107, 141, 143
appointment panels 137-41
  see also selection and recruitment
assent to decisions 89
assessment see evaluation and monitoring
attention spans 43-4
attentiveness 8-10
Attlee, Clement 17, 88
audio(visual) conferences 149-52
auditing
  audit committees 100, 103, 111
  of accounts 126
  of board members' skills 117
authority 36-7, 77, 80, 87
autocratic behaviour 7, 13, 41-2, 73, 87-8
'away days' 34, 76, 147, 151

Bales, Robert Freed 37-8
ballots 124, 127
banking crisis (2008-09) 109
behaviour of groups 35-8
  see also aggression, autocratic behaviour, conflict in meetings, consensus in meetings, dissent from decisions, fairness, 'groupthink', interruptions in meetings, non-verbal communication, respect, trust

Bierce, Ambrose 82
bilingual meetings 147-9
boards 95-117
    agendas and papers 50
body language 9-10, 150
Bono, Edward de 85, 145-6
Bradbury, Malcolm 43
brainstorming 85, 146
businesses *see* companies
Buzan, Tony 85

Cabinet, UK government 17, 32,
    87-8
candidates, interview 137-41
casting vote of chairs 124
chairs (furniture) 52, 59-60
challenging thinking
    at annual meetings 124
    by chairs 15, 37, 75, 79, 106
    by boards 104, 110
    by facilitators 145, 147
charisma, limited value of 16
charities 97-101
    accountability of 24
    legal responsibilities 114
charters 97, 99
Checkland, Peter 85
chief executives 95-117
    authority 36
    relationship with chairs 25
Churchill, Winston 17
closed sessions, board meetings
    112
committees, of boards 98, 100,
    103, 110
    *see also* audit committees,
    nomination committees
communication with group
    members 41, 49-51, 93, 100,
    103
    *see also* non-verbal
    communication
companies
    boards 101-105
    duties of chairs 25
company secretaries 104
competences *see* skills and
        expertise
compromising 80
computers in meetings 50, 52,
    62
concluding meetings 91-2, 132,
    136
conferences 128-32
    *see also* teleconferences,
    'unconferences',
    videoconferences
confidence *see* trust
conflict in meetings 36, 53, 54,
    79, 82-3, 87, 114, 136
    *see also* dissent from decisions
consensus in meetings 36, 74,
    79-80, 87, 104, 144, 145
    *see also* assent to decisions,
    compromising, consent to
    decisions, conviction about
    decisions, 'groupthink'
consent to decisions 89
consistency, of chairs 12
constitution of boards 97, 110
consulting group members 41
conversations, in meetings 81,
    84, 152
conviction about decisions 89
corrections to minutes 65, 92-3
co-opting group members 32, 34

dates of next meetings 34, 48,
    91
debate *see* discussion
decisions and decision-making
    86-91
    by boards 114
    by groups 5-6
    chairs to secure 18, 19, 54
    contrary to chair's views 74
    rules for 121
    *see also* consensus in meetings,
    implementing decisions, voting
declarations of interest 47
delegation
    by boards 111
    by chairs 41, 78, 90, 93
deputy chairs 20

development *see* training and development
'devil's advocate', chairs as 79, 83, 140
dictatorial behaviour 7, 13, 41-2, 73, 87-8
digressions in discussion 76, 84
directors, company board 101-105
disabled group members 31, 51, 52, 53
disciplinary hearings and procedures 107, 141-3
discussions *see* participation in discussions, steering discussions, summing up discussions
dissent from decisions 74, 88-9
diversity of group members 30-31, 103
division of responsibilities, between chairs and chief executives 101-102, 104, 105-107
documentation *see* agendas, papers, reports and reporting
duration
  of groups 25, 42-4
  of meetings 42-4, 46, 152

effectiveness of meetings 92, 116-17
election of officers 124, 127
electronic documents 50
empathetic skills 10-12
environment of meetings 51-3
equipment for meetings 52-3, 129, 149-52
  *see also* microphones
'Erskine May' 121
evaluation and monitoring
  of boards 103, 110-11, 116-17
  of chairs 102, 117
  of chief executives 103
  of job applicants 139-40
  of meetings 93

evidence 5, 18, 66, 76, 87, 143
executive directors 102, 103
executives *see* chief executives
expertise *see* skills and expertise
extraordinary general meetings (EGMs) 128

facilitating 116, 144-7
fairness 12-13, 98, 114, 135, 141-2
'false compromise' 80
'false consensus' 80
feeding back to meetings 9, 14, 147
finance
  monitoring 110, 111
  responsibilities of boards 97, 98, 103
  responsibilities of chairs 25
Financial Reporting Council 101, 102
'fishbowls' 128
following up meetings 92-3, 114-15, 140
formal meetings xiii, 69, 82, 88, 113-14, 121-4
functions of chairs 18-19
fundraising 100, 115

gender differences
  in meetings 37-8
  on company boards 103
governance of boards 97, 101-103, 105-106, 110, 116
grievance hearings and procedures 107, 141-7
groups
  behaviour 35-8
  benefits and drawbacks 3-6
  communication within 49-51
  decision taking 5-6
  duration 25, 42-4
  dynamics 35-6
  exploratory 5
  formation 4-6, 15, 35-6
  maintenance of 18
  members 28-34, 77-8

place and time 42
social interactions 6, 35-6
terminology xiv
terms of reference 26-8
training of members 33, 100,
104-105, 113, 117
types 24-5
see also appointment panels,
boards, Cabinet, charities,
committees of boards,
companies, conferences, Privy
Council, public boards, small
groups, task groups
'groupthink' 29, 79-80, 109

heckling 133, 135-6
House of Commons (UK)
adjournment of debates 84
rules of debate 121

icebreaking 145
impartiality of chairs 12-13,
144
implementing decisions 89-91,
93, 108
see also action points
imposing decisions 87-8
improving
chairing skills 155
meeting effectiveness 92,
116-17
independence
of board members 100, 105
of chairs 23
independent non-executive
directors 102-103
induction see training and
development
information sharing 41, 86, 106,
108, 113
inquorate meetings 121
inspiring group members 16
integrity 12-13
interaction process analysis 37
interest, declaring 47
internet access in meetings 50,
52, 62

interruptions in meetings 38,
133, 135-6
interventions by chairs in
discussion 55, 73, 75-86
interviews, job 137-41
introducing meetings 53, 60-63,
126, 129, 135

Janis, Irving 79
job interviews 137-41
joint chairs 7-8

knowledge see skills and
expertise

language, in meetings 147-9
see also body language
leadership skills xi, 15-17, 101,
156
legal responsibilities
of board 97-8, 114
of chairs 25, 137, 141
see also rules and regulations
length see duration
listening skills 8-10
see also attention spans
location of meetings 42, 46,
51-3

Mackintosh, John 88
Marks & Spencer 102
'matters arising' 47-8, 53, 64-6
media
invited to public meetings 134
reporting of company annual
meetings 104
representation of companies
105
role of chairs 115
skills 16
meetings
alternatives to 41
benefits and drawbacks 3-6
boards 112-15
company boards 104
conducting 57-93
decision making 5-6

exploratory 5
preparing for 39-60
reasons for calling 4-6
reputation of xi-xii
social interactions 6, 35-6
time spent in 4
see also annual meetings, 'away
days', bilingual meetings,
conferences, formal meetings,
political meetings, public
meetings, remote meetings
men, speaking in meetings 37-8
mentors, in chairing skills 19,
20, 117
microphones 52, 130, 134, 152
'mind maps' (Tony Buzan) 85
minutes 63, 64-6
agenda item 47
dissent noted 74, 88-9
minute-taking 35, 64, 92-3
publishing 93
recording decisions 74, 88-9
summaries 93, 113
monitoring see evaluation and
monitoring
motions 121-2
multilingual meetings 147-9

networking 12-13, 115
see also social networking
neutrality 144
'next business' motions 123
'Nolan rules' 98-9
nominal group technique 146
nomination committees 103, 105
nominations for elections 125,
127
non-departmental public bodies
99
non-executive directors 102-104
non-experts 17
non-participants in meetings 10,
37, 77, 81-2, 89
non-verbal communication 10,
38, 150
note-taking by chairs 75
notice

of 'any other business' 69
of meetings 49-51, 125
of motions 121-2

objectives
of groups 26-8
of meetings 61, 62
objectivity of chairs 12-13, 144
observing other chairs 20, 155
open sessions, in board meetings
112
openness, between chairs and
chief executives 106, 107
options appraisal 79, 87
orchestrating discussions 14, 15-
16, 18, 54, 63-4, 73-86, 134

panels
appointment 137-40
of speakers 132, 134, 135
papers for meetings 49-51, 66-7,
113, 125, 149
see also agendas, minutes,
reports
parent bodies 24, 93
Parkinson's Law 42
Parliament (UK)
adjournment of debates 84
rules of debate 121
participation in discussion,
encouraging 74-5, 77-8, 81-2,
145-7
patience, in chairs 14
payment to chairs 98, 99
performance see evaluation and
monitoring
physiological environment of
meetings 51-3
place of meetings 42, 46, 51-3
planning meetings see preparing
for meetings
points of order 123
political meetings 128, 130-1,
132-3
postponing discussion 66, 84
see also adjournment of
debates and meetings

power within groups 36-7
preparing for meetings 39-60
  annual meetings 125
  appointment panels 137-8
  boards 104, 112-13
  conferences 128-9
  disciplinary and grievance
    hearings 141-2
  facilitation 144-7
  public meetings 133-5
presentations to meetings 67,
  112, 138
press *see* media
Prime Ministers 17, 88
principles of public life 99
Privy Council 52
promptness, in starting meetings
  60
proposing motions 121-2
proxies 126
public access to minutes 93
public boards 25, 97-101
public meetings 112, 124,
  132-6
public speaking 115
publicising meetings 125, 134

Quakers (Society of Friends) 7
quasi-judicial hearings 141-3
'question be put' motions 123
questionnaires 41, 116, 132
questions
  annual meetings 104
  put by chairs to group members
    74, 82
  put to job applicants 137-9
  public meetings 134, 135
  to conference speakers 130-31
quorum 121, 126

recommendations 5, 24, 27,
  68, 78
record of meetings 53, 75
  *see also* minutes
recruitment *see* selection and
  recruitment
redaction of minutes 93

Rees-Mogg, William 43
refreshments in meetings 53
regulations *see* rules and
  regulations
remote meetings 42, 149-52
remuneration of chairs 98, 99
reports and reporting
  by chairs 24, 93
  to meetings 48, 67-8, 147
  *see also* annual reports, media
representativeness of group
  members 30-31, 103, 116
representing the group
  role of boards 110, 111-12
  role of chairs 16, 115
  *see also* media
resolutions 127
respect
  between chairs and chief
    executives 106
  for group members 13
'rich pictures' (Peter Checkland)
  85
risk monitoring 103, 110, 111
role play 19, 145-6
rooms, meeting 51-3
Rose, Stuart 102
rules and regulations 55, 77, 99,
  106, 110, 114, 121, 124-5,
  141
  *see also* legal responsibilities,
    standing orders

scoring *see* evaluation and
  monitoring
seating in meetings 52, 59-60
seconding motions 122
secretaries
  annual meetings 125
  as preparation for becoming
    chairs 20
  attentiveness 9
  roles 34-5
  seating position in meeting 60
  setting agenda 15, 44, 48
  taking minutes 35, 64-5, 75,
    92-3

terminology xiv
*see also* company secretaries
selection and recruitment
of chairs 23-4, 32, 98, 102,
103
of chief executives 106, 109
of group members 28-32, 105,
110, 117
*see also* appointment panels
'Seven Principles of Public Life'
99
shareholders 102, 103, 104,
128
silent group members 10, 37,
77, 81-2, 89
simultaneous translation 53,
129, 148
'Six Thinking Hats' (Edward de
Bono) 85, 145-6
skills and expertise
audit of board members' skills
117
of chairs 8-19
of group members 36, 55,
100, 105, 110, 116
of job applicants 137, 139,
140
small groups 85, 146
SMART formula 26
social networking 134
Society of Friends ('Quakers') 7
Speaker (House of Commons) 82
speakers
addressing the chair 82, 122
annual meetings 126
conferences 129-32
public meetings 134, 135
*see also* presentations to
meetings, public speaking,
silent group members,
troublesome group members
staff meetings 133
standing orders 99, 121, 123
status, within groups 36-7
steering discussions 14,
15-16, 18, 54, 63-4, 73-86,
134

strategy of boards 103, 105,-
106, 107, 110, 116
styles of chairing 55
subordinate bodies 24, 67, 78
*see also* committees, of boards
substantive motions 122
summing up discussions 14, 67,
84-5, 86, 122, 132, 147
support to chief executives
by chairs 105-109
by boards 110, 111
surveys of group members 41,
116-17, 132
sympathy 10

tables for meetings 52, 59-60
task groups 25
teleconferences 149-52
tellers 124, 127
terms of reference 26-8
thanking group members 54, 91,
93, 127-8, 132
'through the chair', speaking 82,
122
time and timekeeping
duration of meetings 42-4, 46
facilitation sessions 147
overrunning 15, 67, 130, 131
promptness in starting
meetings 60
sending out papers for meetings
50
time of day for meetings 51
time spent in meetings 4, 100-
101
timekeeping in meetings 63-4,
67, 76-9, 122, 130
timing of meetings 34, 42, 51,
112
trade union meetings 133
training and development
media training 115
of chairs 19-20, 155-6
of group members 33, 99-100,
104-105, 113, 117
*see also* mentors, skills and
expertise

translation, simultaneous 53,
129, 148
treasurer 48, 67, 100, 126
troublesome group members 14,
82-3, 131, 135-6
trust 12, 36, 90, 106, 107,
111, 151
trusts *see* charities
Tuckman, Bruce 35-6

UK Corporate Governance Code
102, 116
'unconferences' 128
universities, meetings in 43, 113

values
of chairs 12, 106

of groups 103, 105, 107, 110
vice-chairs 20, 100
videoconferences 149-52
Voice over Internet Protocol
(VoIP) 150
volunteer group members 3, 28
votes of thanks 132
voting 14, 83,87, 89, 114, 122,
124, 126, 127

Wales, bilingual meetings 148-9
welcoming group members 47,
53, 59, 61, 113, 126, 129
women
representation on company
boards 103
speaking in meetings 37-8

# artist **Juta Tirona** illustrator

# Contact

www.jutatirona.com
juta.tirona@gmail.com

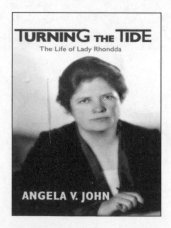